Dedication

This book is dedicated to the faithful and committed members of Progressive Baptist Convention, Inc. May God continue to bless our leaders and lay people as we collectively strive to uphold out tradition of social justice and divinely inspired preaching. Lastly, this book is dedicated to the memory and legacy of our Dean of Preaching – Gardner Calvin Taylor.

Dr. Taylor, we will not let you down. We promise to *Just Preach!*

Acknowledgement

On behalf of President Dr. James Perkins, the staff of MMGI Books would like to thank the contributors of this book for their willingness to submit a sermon that reflects the rich tradition of Progressive National Baptist preaching prowess. In addition, we would like to acknowledge and thank the Executive Assistants of the contributors. Many of them received directives from their pastors as it pertains to this project late in the production process. This project was only made possible because of the Grace of God and the calculating vision of our capable President Perkins. Therefore, the staff of MMGI Books acknowledges the favor of God via both the vertical and horizontal axis of His matchless power and His unyielding grace.

Darryl D. Sims

MANUSCRIPT MANAGEMENT GROUP, INC.
THE PATH TO PUBLICATION

- *Do you want to publish a book?*
- *Would you like your book published in 90 days?*
- *Would you like a free consultation from the Publishing Coach?*

If so, continue to read this ad and contact our publishing team at 773.314.7060.

Who We Are

Manuscript Management Group, Inc. (MMGI) is the vision of founder and president, Rev. Darryl D. Sims. After self-publishing several of his own works, Rev. Sims realized that several of his colleagues wanted to know how he did it. Seeing the need and seizing the opportunity, Rev. Sims formed MMGI. It is the primary goal of MMGI to fulfill a need within the Christian community to provide quality, Christian-based book packaging services targeted toward pastors, church leaders, and Christian educators.

What We Do

MMGI, is a book packaging company. Most writers have heard of book packagers, but few have actually worked with them and have seen first-hand what they do. The fact is, having a finished manuscript is the beginning of the book packaging process.

Unlike any other players in the publishing industry, book packagers are specifically equipped to devote the time, energy, and focused attention necessary to bring your project(s) to fruition-through manuscript development, editorial production and graphic design, guiding your project to publication. Drawing on the most sophisticated design and production technologies, book packagers can handle every stage of the publishing process and be counted upon to deliver a product on schedule with the highest level of professionalism.

Perhaps you are a great writer with an excellent project (sermon or manuscript), but you lack the editorial acumen or don't know how to begin to find an editor, graphic designer, or printer. MMGI can fill these specific holes. Suppose you need help developing specific concepts or turning your sermon series in to a well-formed teaching tool to meet the needs of your congregation, MMGI can help. As a book packager, it is our goal to help you as the author, guide your manuscript along the path to publication.

MMGI: The Path to Publication

Just Preach!
Proclaiming the Word of God...
  Progressive National Baptist Style

MMGI BOOKS, CHICAGO, ILLINOIS

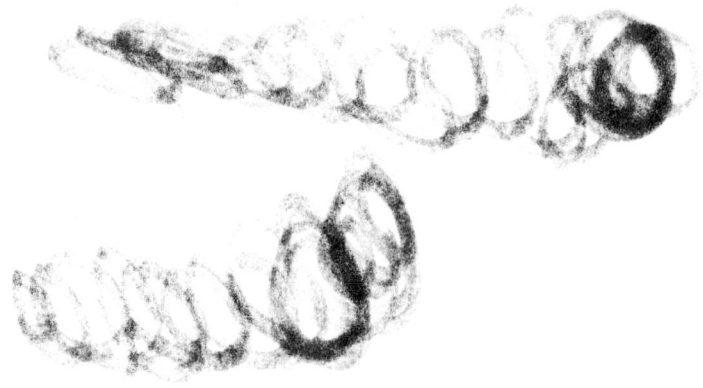

Published by MMGI Books, Chicago, IL 60636
www.mmgibooks.com

JUST PREACH! Proclaiming the Word of God... Progressive National Baptist Style
Copyright © 2015 by MMGI BOOKS

All rights reserved. No part of this publication may be reproduced, stored in a retrieval system, or transmitted in any form or by any means, electronic, mechanical, photocopying, recording, or otherwise, without the prior permission of the copyright owner, except for brief quotations included in a review of the book.

Except for quotations from Scripture, the quoted ideas expressed in the book are not, in all cases, exact quotations, as some have been edited for clarity and brevity. In all cases, the author has attempted to maintain the speaker's original intent. In some cases, quoted material for this book was obtained from secondary sources, primarily print media. While every effort was made to ensure the accuracy of these sources, the accuracy cannot be guaranteed. For additions, deletions, corrections, or classifications in future editions of this text, please write Manuscript Management Group, Inc.

Scriptures marked NIV are from the Holy Bible, New International Version, Copyright © 1973, 1978, 1984 by International Bible Society. Used by permission of Zondervan Publishing House. All rights reserved.

Scriptures by NKJV are taken from the New King James Version. Copyright © 1982 by Thomas Nelson, Inc. Used by permission. All rights reserved

Scriptures marked NLT are taken from the Holy Bible, New Living Translation, copyright © 1996. Used by permission of Tyndale House Publisher's, Inc. Wheaton, Illinois 60189. All rights reserved.

Scriptures marked KJV are taken from the King James Version.

Library of Congress Cataloging-in-Publication Data

Just Preach: Proclaiming the Word Progressive National Baptist Style

p. cm

ISBN 978-1-939774-18-7

Religious life. 2. General public – Conduct of life. 3. Christian – Development. MMGI BOOKS

Printed in the U.S.A.

Table of Contents

Introduction iv

Humble Beginnings iv

A Look At The Elders Of Antioch Marvin A. McMickle 1

There Is Life In The Valley William. H. Robinson 9

Stronger In My Broken Places Charles E. Booth 17

How To Survive With Seven Skinny Cows When The Economy Is Shot James C. Perkins 29

On Breaking Through Barriers Raphael G. Warnock 41

A Divine Deterrent Delores James Cain 45

A Dialogue With Death Johnny R. Youngblood 53

Learning To Let It Go Tyrone P. Jones IV 63

Good News In A Culture of Violence: How To Stop A Funeral Procession Earl B. Payton 69

A Risk Of Faith Gina M. Stewart 75

Standing Firm In Critical Times: Our God Is Able Kenneth J. Flowers 83

Don't Give Up On Jesus Willie R. Davis 89

Born To Do It Jacqueline A. Thompson 93

The Encouragement Of Adversity Charlie Dates 101

Beating the Giants That Beat Our Fathers Anthony M. Chandler 107

You Can't Tell What Prayer Can Do E. Winford Bell 115

INTRODUCTION

This book is a celebration of African American preaching in the Progressive National Baptist Tradition. Three generations of preaching are represented in this volume of *Just Preach!* with sermon contributions written and others composed by pastors of varying educational backgrounds. Each of the sixteen preachers in this book have, throughout their preaching careers, demonstrated a ready acumen for biblical interpretation and revealed undeniable strength in communicating the Gospel. I am sure the sermons comprised in this book will help satisfy the inquisitive preacher in need of a sermon book with varied homiletic styles, assist the everyday believer who wishes to receive a divinely inspired Word, and minister to everyone with a desire to hear devoted messengers of the Gospel. All of the contributors undeniably possess the ability to Just Preach!

While every preacher shares the essential task of simply bringing God's Word to life, each of them is gifted with a unique voice and particular style to convey it. The varying homiletic styles of the Progressive National Baptist preacher are as nuanced as our national demography. These styles vary between each state, region, and local community. Yet, among this diverse sector of Christianity, there is a unifying thread woven throughout the history of our church that persists until this very moment. This dynamic and prolific thread is the notion of 'social activism' within our preaching. The Progressive National Baptist preachers are known worldwide for their preaching prowess and social consciousness. Many of them follow in the tradition of Dr. Martin Luther King, Jr.

HUMBLE BEGINNINGS

The Progressive National Baptist Convention, Inc. (PNBC) started as a movement reflecting the religious, social and political climate of its time. Its mission was to transform the traditional African American Baptist Convention as well as society. The formation of the convention was wrapped up in the Civil Rights Movement and was begun by some of the same persons who were deeply involved in the freedom movement for African Americans in the United States. Even though the seeds of the convention were sown by discontent with the lack of democratic process within the National Baptist Convention, U.S.A Inc. (NBCUSA Inc.), the roots of its development went far beyond issues of tenure of office and leadership.

One of the visionaries of this era who challenged the NBCUSA, Inc. was the Rev. L. Venchael Booth who envisioned a new convention that was progressive and forward thinking, a convention that would respond to the spiritual and social needs of the time.

In a response to a letter sent out by the Rev. Booth, 33 delegates from 14 states met November 14-15, 1961 at his church, the Zion Baptist Church in Cincinnati, Ohio. The Rev. J. Raymond Henderson, pastor of Second Baptist Church of Los Angeles, California, presided over the meeting. As a result of this two-day intensive organizational meeting, the Progressive National Baptist Convention Inc. was formed.

As a result of that founding meeting, the Rev. T. M. Chambers was elected as its first President. Leadership from across the United States joined the Progressive Baptist family and spawned the Progressive National Baptist Movement. Issues of freedom, civil and human rights, and progressive ideas became the cornerstone for the convention. The PNBC became a new Christian movement which included an array of social and political concerns embodied in its founding principles of Fellowship, Progress, Peace and Service.

The PNBC movement was under girded by Dr. Martin Luther King Jr.'s struggle for freedom for African Americans. It was the PNBC that provided a denominational home for Dr. Martin Luther King Jr. and many of the Baptist leaders in the Civil Rights Movement. They all became important forces in the life and work of the Progressive National Baptist Convention, Inc.

As a result of this involvement from members of the Civil Rights Movement the centerpiece of the PNBC witness became one of social justice and human liberation as a mandate of the Gospel. In essence, the PNBC became a living African American Christian organism, vibrant with energy and committed to the social gospel for the transformation of U.S. society.

Since its beginning, the PNBC has always been ecumenical, supporting the World Council of Churches, the National Council of Churches, the Baptist World Alliance and other ecumenical bodies. The PNBC is actively engaged in national and international ministries in Africa, Asia, Europe, Latin America and the Caribbean as well as the United States of America.

In the United States there are PNBC churches in 35 states. The membership of the PNBC is primarily urban with some of the most noted churches in urban cities. The membership of the convention comes from many different social classes and strata. A large percentage of PNBC churches are engaged in urban programs that focus on the youth, the elderly, housing, economic development and prison ministries. The convention has a pension program and the Nannie Helen Burroughs School is establishing schools internationally.

Reference
https://en.wikipedia.org/wiki/Progressive_National_Baptist_Convention

A Look At The Elders Of Antioch
Marvin A. McMickle, Ph.D.
Acts 11: 18-26 and 13: 1-3

From the moment I entered the ministry in 1971, nearly 40 years ago, I have had the opportunity to work in churches whose very name carried great biblical or historical significance. When I first began, I served at Bethany Baptist Church in Brooklyn, New York. That church was named for the village outside of Jerusalem where Jesus spent so much time with Mary, Martha and their brother, Lazarus. Two years later I went to Abyssinian Baptist Church in New York City. This church was named after the ancient North African nation that is now called Ethiopia. Moreover the church was actually founded in 1808 by merchant marines, professional commercial sailors who frequently docked in New York City. Abyssinian or Ethiopia was one of the earliest centers of the Christian faith. The eunuch who served Queen Candace, who was converted to Christianity under the ministry of the apostle Philip, came from that region of the world. It is believed that the Ethiopian Coptic Church is centuries older than the Roman Catholic Church centered in Italy.

In 1976, I went to St. Paul Baptist Church in Montclair, New Jersey. That church was, of course, named for the great apostle who established so many of the early churches and wrote almost one half of the books in the New Testament. Since 1987 I have served here at the Antioch Baptist Church of Cleveland, Ohio. Our church is named after that community of Christians who lived in the city of Antioch as discussed in Acts 13. Antioch was a city north of Jerusalem in what is modern day Syria. Antioch, along with Jerusalem, Ephesus and Rome, was one of the great cities of the Roman Empire and one of the early centers of the Christian faith. In fact, according to Acts 11: 26, it was in Antioch that the followers of Jesus were first called Christians.

It was from the city of Antioch that Paul began his first missionary journey to the Gentile nations (Acts 13: 2-4). Moreover, it was in Antioch that the first great conflict of the church was finally resolved; whether or not Gentile converts to Christianity would be required to submit to the Jewish ritual of circumcision and conform to a kosher diet (Acts 15: 22-31). While the decision about gentiles was decided in Jerusalem that decision was first announced and enacted in Antioch. I hope you find it as interesting as I do that our church in Cleveland is a living reminder of the importance of the Christian church that existed in the city of Antioch in Syria almost 2,000 years ago.

However, there is something just as interesting and just as important about the church in the city of Antioch, something that historians and filmmakers seem to have overlooked or completely ignored. It has to do with the ethnic and cultural and regional composition of the church in Antioch 2000 years ago. Acts 13 mentions the names of four men who were among the elders, or spiritual leaders, of that early Christian community. People from all over the world are quite familiar with two of those names; Barnabas and Saul. Every Sunday school student has heard something about both of those apostles. Their names are just as well known to us as the names of the Lord's first disciples Peter, James and John and the others.

However, there were two other names mentioned in Acts 13 that seem to have been completely forgotten, or overlooked, or relegated to the trash heap of history. Nevertheless, there they are for all to notice; Simeon who was called Niger and Lucius of Cyrene. Who do you suppose these two men were, and what is important to us about their presence in the Bible? Simeon was called Niger. That is a Latin word that means black or dark. So we know there was a leader in the church at Antioch whose skin color was so conspicuous that he was called Niger. He was a black man in the language of the modern day.

The other man was Lucius from Cyrene. That was a city from the North African country that is now known as Libya. This is not the first time a man from Cyrene entered the New Testament story. You will remember that it was a man named Simon of Cyrene who was forced to carry the cross of Jesus when the Lord could no longer stand beneath the awful weight of that implement of execution. Now we meet another man named Lucius from that same African country. Consider that the leaders of the church at Antioch not only included the two well known characters of Paul and Barnabas, but also included one man who was referred to as Niger and another man whose homeland is identified as the region of North Africa.

Do you not find it strange that these names are seldom if ever mentioned in most churches? Saul and Barnabas have churches, schools and hospitals named after them. Meanwhile, nothing has been done to establish forever the names of Simeon the Niger and Lucius of Cyrene. Let me point out to you that these two men and their ethnic identity were not inserted into the Bible long after the book of Acts had been completed. They were not an afterthought. Their names were not inserted in the Bible during the Civil Rights Movement. There was no U.S. Supreme Court order that mandated that these names be included as a form of Affirmative Action. These names, and the link they certify between black people and biblical faith, have been in the Book of Acts from the beginning. But for all of this time they have been largely overlooked, if not completely ignored. It is important for us to **Take a Look at the Elders of Antioch.**

Let me state several reasons why this observation is important, especially now at the start of our annual observance of Black History Month. First of all, this single text helps us dispel the Gospel according to Cecil B. De Mille, the Hollywood filmmaker. Has it ever occurred to you that all of his epic films about biblical stories relegate black people to obscurity? Consider the most notable example of excluding black people from the biblical story which would have been *The Ten Commandments*. How likely do you think it is that Moses really looked like Charlton Heston, or that Rameses I looked like Yul Brynner? Not a single person who appeared in that film as an ancient Egyptian bore even the slightest resemblance to what we know was the appearance of ancient Egyptians.

Of course, Cecil B. DeMille did have the nation of Ethiopia represented in that film. The Egyptians had just conquered them, and the proud black actor, Woody Strode, played their king. How odd that all the Ethiopians (conquered people) were portrayed by black people, while all the Egyptians (conquerors) were played by whites. Those two nations share a common border, and they live beneath the sun equatorial sun, so how they could look so different from one another is more a matter of the racism of Hollywood in 1958 than a matter of historical accuracy. What filmmakers cannot undo in 1958 is what we see written here in Acts 13 that dates to around 60 AD. The Gospel according to Cecil B. DeMille is not the Authorized Version. Black people have played a leading role in the Bible for thousands of years. So my first point is simply the matter of historical accuracy and the presence of black people in the Bible as far back as the ancient Egyptians and Ethiopians right up to Simon the Niger and Lucius of Cyrene in Acts 13.

A second equally important point for us, especially during Black History Month, is the reminder that our history as a people does not begin in the cotton fields and tobacco patches of North and South America and the Caribbean. Long before we came to this hemisphere, African people had established countries and great civilizations. References to such places as Egypt, Ethiopia, and Cyrene remind us of that fact. We have all heard about the great Roman Empire, but we have heard almost nothing about the black general named Hannibal, from the North African city of Carthage, who conquered Rome in one of the single greatest military maneuvers of all time. Slavery in America may be part of the history of some African people, but our history certainly does not begin at that point.

You are not fully aware of this fact until you go to Africa and discover that they are almost completely disinterested in the issue of slavery in America. Remember, however, that the people now living in Africa are largely the descendants of people who were never taken from their homelands. They are the offspring of the people who escaped the snare of the slave catchers and the suffering of the Middle Passage. The people of Africa are much more interested in shaking off the last vestiges of European colonial rule on the African continent that ended just forty years ago, than they are in what happened to those Africans who were taken away, never to return, four hundred years ago.

When you go to Africa you become reconnected to the cultures that existed on that continent while Europe was still groping through the Dark Ages. Empires ,such as Songhay and Mali were centers of art, learning and organized religion long before the Trans-Atlantic slave trade began. A recent exhibit at the Cleveland Art Museum focused on the arts and crafts of the West African nation of Benin in the 16th century. That exhibit was a clear and tangible expression that the people of West Africa who were forcibly brought to this country were not savages who needed to be brought to Europe and America in order to save them from the darkness. They were a civilized and ordered community whose darkness only began when they were forced into slavery. Let it never be forgotten that our history does not begin in America, it is rooted in the continent of Africa. This is one of the most important things we can teach during Black History Month. The presence of Simeon the Niger and Lucius of Cyrene is also a reminder of that fact.

A third reason why I am intrigued by the presence of Simeon and Lucius, is that it helps me refute those who continue to insist that Christianity is "the white man's religion", and that Islam is the true religion of the black man. Those of us who grew up in the 60s will remember how many times we heard that from those who followed the teachings of Elijah Muhammad and Malcolm X. They would frequently point to a hangman's noose attached to one of the cross beams of a cross. They would suggest that it was white Christians who were responsible for the brutality inflicted upon black people over the years. That point may be largely true. However, it does not dismiss the presence of Simon and Lucius as leaders of the church at Antioch.

Black people, African people, have been a part of the Christian faith from the very beginning. In fact, the Ethiopian Orthodox Church, sometimes called the Coptic Church, precedes the birth of Islam by over 500 years. Black scholars such as Augustine and Tertullian were helping to shape the doctrines of the Christian faith 400 years before their prophet, Muhammad, had even been born. Islam began in the 8th century AD, but Simon the Niger and Lucius of Cyrene were serving on the ordination council that dispatched Paul and Barnabas on their first missionary journey in the 1st century. Does that sound like a white man's religion to you?

I do not doubt and I cannot refute the claim that much of the worst that had happened during slavery was done with the full knowledge and support of some organized groups of white Christians. However, many white Christians also fought and died to end slavery both in America and in Europe. It must also be noted that the African slave trade involved Muslim slave traders who cooperated in the capture and exportation of black Africans not only West to the Americas, but also East to the Arabian Peninsula.

There is enough blame to go around so far as the active participation of both Muslims and Christians in the slave trade is concerned. But the main point must be kept clear. Black people are not out of touch with their history when they confess faith in Jesus Christ. They have been doing that since Simeon the Niger and Lucius of Cyrene were among the elders at Antioch in the 1st century A.D.

My fourth and final point is this; the story in Acts 13 must serve as a challenge to the modern day Christian church around the world. You and I are members of a church that carries the name of the place where people were first called Christians. Wouldn't it be great of we looked and acted like those whose name we bear into the 21st century? It seems that racism has caused us to digress from the organizational style of the church at Antioch. Notice that Saul and Barnabas, along with Simon and Lucius served as leaders in that church. How many churches today have leadership that looks like that? Not many, I would imagine. Rather than having inter-racial leadership, we can barely sustain a handful of inter-racial memberships in our churches across the country. The words of Liston Pope, so often quoted by Dr. King, remain true to this day. "Eleven o'clock Sunday morning is the most segregated hour of the week in America." It was not always so. In the church at Antioch, there were Paul and Barnabas, and there was also Simeon and Lucius. How sad that we have reverted to our present state of racial separation.

Let us use the reminder of Ecclesiastes, that there is nothing new under the sun (1:9). Integrating our churches is not something we need to attempt to do for the first time in the 21st century. It is something that we need to reclaim from the church at Antioch in the very 1st century A.D. And we must remember that integration is not the real issue. The real issue is the equality of all persons. When Paul in Acts 17 says to the Greeks in Athens, "From one blood God made all nations of men to dwell together on the face of the earth", he may have had his friendship with Simeon and Lucius on his mind. When he said in Galatians 3, "There is neither Jew nor Gentile..." he might have had Simeon and Lucius on his mind.

I am not interested in arguing that Simeon and Lucius were better than Saul and Barnabas. I am not interested in proving that they were smarter or more faithful than Saul and Barnabas. I just want you and the rest of the world to know that they were in this story about Christ from the very beginning. I want to write them back into the telling of the history of the early church. I want us to be aware of all the people who were numbered among the elders at Antioch. It is not too much to say that the words of Jesus apply even in this case; "You shall know the truth and the truth shall set you free (John 8:32). Antioch was the place where the followers of Jesus were first called Christians, and the leadership in that church consisted not only of Paul and Barnabas but also Simon the Niger and Lucius of Cyrene.

What should be true in the church should also be true in the world. God is not the author of division or discrimination. God did not decree that people live in separated and segregated positions within society. Our service of communion speaks directly to the intentions of the God who placed Paul and Barnabas as well as Simon and Lucius in the same church. There is something known as "closed communion" where people are intentionally excluded from sharing in communion with other believers if they do not share precisely the same view as regards certain doctrines and beliefs. There have been some Baptist churches that have held this view. Thankfully, most Baptists practice something known as "open communion." That means that all baptized believers in Jesus Christ are welcome to come to this table when we share the bread and wine together. No one is overlooked or excluded because of race or doctrine or denominational differences.

How sad that this is not yet not true with all Christian bodies. There are some Christian groups that only invite members of their denomination to share in communion. There are some churches where communion is official only if a priest or pastor within that group presides at the table. Otherwise, some people will not come forward. How and why have we built these self-imposed divisions among ourselves? How did we get to this state of disunity? Surely the church of the 21st century can learn from the church of the 1st century when it comes to diversity and inclusion. I wonder today if the Christians in Antioch in the 21st century are faithfully carrying on the tradition of the Christians in Antioch of the 1st century. May our congregation always be a place where Paul and Barnabas along with Simon the Niger and Lucius of Cyrene can sit and serve together.

We might as well learn how to live, and work, and worship down here on earth, because the Bible says nothing about separate sections in heaven. There will be no black section over here and no white section over there. There will be no all-male section over here and all-women over there. There will not even be a Baptist section over here for those that have been through the baptism of bodily immersion in water, and no Methodist section over there for those that have been "dry cleaned." I love the chorus that says:

> *When we all get to heaven,*
> *What a day of rejoicing that will be.*
> *When we all see Jesus,*
> *We'll sing and shout the victory.*

I know the story of John Street Methodist Episcopal Church in New York City in 1796. I know about Peter Williams, Sr. and James Varick who stood up for the right of black clergy to exercise their gifts for ministry that the white Methodist Episcopal Church had disallowed. I know what happened in 1821, when The African Methodist Episcopal Zion Church was organized. I know that the AME Zion Church has been called the Freedom Church, because Frederick Douglass, Sojourner Truth, Harriet Tubman, and Paul Robeson were shaped and molded in the Zion Church. I know all of that, and I honor and salute all of that.

However, I know one thing more. I know about the church at Antioch in Syria. I know they were first called Christians there. They commissioned Paul and Barnabas to their ministry as missionaries for Jesus Christ. And I know that on that ordination council, among the elders at Antioch were two black men; Simeon the Niger and Lucius of Cyrene. If the church had kept their names alive, history would have been very different. We would have known about the black presence in the Bible. We would have known that our history did not begin in slavery, but with great and cultured societies in Africa. We would have known that there were black Christians 700 years before the prophet Muhammad was born. Finally, we would have known that from the Day of Pentecost in Acts to the commissioning of Paul and Barnabas in Acts 13, the church of Jesus Christ began as an inter- racial and as an inter-cultural community. I do not know if we will ever get back to that kind of church.

I do know this, however, that this life is not all there is for those who put our faith in Christ. I know that God has something waiting for the faithful on the other side of this earthly journey. I know that weeping may endure for an evening, but that joy will come in the morning. And in that heavenly home, in that house not made with hands, there will be the descendants of Paul and Barnabas, and the descendants of Simeon the Niger and Lucius of Cyrene. *"When we all get to heaven what a day of rejoicing that will be. When we all see Jesus, we'll sing and shout the victory."*

THERE IS LIFE IN THE VALLEY
William H. Robinson
Ezekiel 37:1-10

We have a report from a Prophet who informs us that he arrived at a strange location - a location where Delta, American Airlines, Swiss Air, and other air carriers could not have landed him, a location where Amtrak could not have taken him by rail. This is a location where no means or form of conventional transportation service could have taken him. My question to the prophet is: "If you did not get there by air, railway, or automobile, how did you come to the region where we find you at the time of our text? Ezekiel says, he got there by means of divine transportation. He says, "The hand of the Lord was upon me and carried me out in the Spirit of the Lord, and set me down in the midst of the valley." Ezekiel begins by telling us, that The Spirit of the Lord took him up and showed him a valley full of dry bones.

If we are going to raise our communities and find resurrection power in our lives we need to move beyond this idea or misnomer that the Spirit only causes us to jump, shout, and have a good time. In fact, I've discovered that in this age of the "charismatic movement" and prosperity gospel, every time we talk about the Spirit, He's making us feel good. He's making us shout, dance, and cry "Hallelujah."

However, what this text seem to suggest is when you are in the midst of a dying people, the Spirit will not allow you to bury your head in the sand and cry "Peace, peace," when there is no peace, and thank God for your prosperity, when your neighborhood is dying, instead the Spirit will show you. In verse1 Ezekiel says, "The Spirit of the Lord took him up." The Spirit didn't take him up to show him all the blessings that were in store for him. It didn't take him up so he could or so he could feel good about himself. The Spirit didn't take him up so he could start seeing all the "stuff" that was going to be his. Instead, the Spirit took him up and said, "Ezekiel, look at what's going on amongst your people and in your neighborhood."

Indeed sometimes the Spirit forces you to deal with the conditions of your people. The Spirit will not allow you to be able to shout in here and then be afraid to walk down the streets once you leave there – But the Spirit will show you. Don't get me wrong, yes, the Spirit will take you up, but sometimes He will bring tears to your eyes once He gets you up. He will show you things about yourself that you didn't even know existed.

Yes, the Spirit will take you up, but sometimes He will have you screaming, "It's not my mother, it's not my father... but it's me O Lord, standing in the need of prayer." God says to Ezekiel, in verse 1, "Ezekiel, are you Spirit-Filled?" Well then, "Come on, I've got something to show you." Look at the violence in our communities. Ezekiel. Ezekiel, look at the homicide rate amongst our youth. Look at the rise of teenage pregnancy in our communities.

Ezekiel, look at those "young brothers" over there who are caught up in a lifestyle of drugs and gangs, along with those "young sisters" who are caught up in a lifestyle of drugs and prostitution. Ezekiel, look at that father over there who's abandoned his family, and that daughter who's been sexually abused and raped. Look at "that mother" who can't sleep at night because her child won't come home – Ezekiel, are you Spirit-filled? Well then, come on, I've got something to show you."

I believe that God is asking us that same question on today: "Are you spirit-filled? Well then, come on, I've got something to show you." He is saying, *I'm not concerned with how well you shout, but I'm concerned with how well you live after you shout. I'm not concerned with how high you jump, but I'm concerned with how straight you walk when you come back down. I'm not concerned with how well you preach, but I want to know if you are you making an impact in somebody's life after you finish preaching. I'm not concerned with how loud you holler, but I want to know if you are helping anybody when you finish hollering* – God is saying, "Are you Spirit-filled? Well then come on, I've got something to show you."

Are you helping anybody as you pass along? Are you cheering somebody with a word or with a song? Are you showing somebody who's traveling wrong? Then your living will not be in vain. Ezekiel says, in verse 1, "God sat him down in the midst of the valley." God didn't even allow Ezekiel to hover over it in a distant observatory where he could do some critical analysis of the predicament give his assessment and then go back to where he usually sits. This text to suggests, that when the Spirit takes you up, it sits you right down in the midst of what you're analyzing. Ezekiel says, "The Spirit sat me in the midst."

The reality is that before you can raise somebody, you have to have some idea of what is going on. You have to know the seriousness of the condition. To do this, you have to analyze the biblical images that are present here, in this text. Contrary to the valley, the geographical location of divine presence is usually the mountain- the place where you get a feel of God, He calls you, and you meet Him. Throughout the Scriptures, God is always showing up on the mountain. Whether it's Mount Sinai, Mount Horeb, Mount Carmel, Mount Nebo, Mount Moriah, or the Mount of Olives the place where God calls you is usually on the Mountain.

However, Ezekiel meets God in a valley. Now in the Scripture, the valley is typically the place, the place of threatened existence. The valley is the place of "God absence." The valley is the place of isolation and a lifeless condition. "The valley" is a biblical term used to help us understand the seriousness of the predicament of a people who were meant to be empowered and alive for God. In fact, God says is essentially saying in this passage, "Children of Israel, you've gotten so weak and so messed up in death. And even though you are My people, who ought to be glorified, a mountain, you're living in the valley instead."

The bones mentioned in verse 1 are the symbol of death: "It was full of bones… and they were scattered all over the place." When we're in a death situation, we start scattering. For example men say they can't work "Women", and "Women say they can't work with "Men." The young say they can't work with the elderly, and the elderly say they can't work with the young. The President says he can't work with the Senate and Senate sys they can't work with the President. The Republicans say they can't work with the Democrats, and the Democrats say they can't work with the Republicans. This civil-rights organization says they can't work with that civil-rights organization. This church says it can't work with that church", and that pastor can't work with this pastor. And if we're not careful, we'll spend more time fighting one another than we will fighting the Enemy. Why? Because we are scattered in a valley!

But then verse 2 says not only were they "scattered in the valley," but they were also "very dry." This geographical setting is an arid region, and one of the fundamental principles of life is water. In fact, every location where they built their communities during this particular time of our text, was around water. The common understanding was this: "Where there is no water, there is no life." God is saying, "Children of Israel, not only are you in a valley, but you are in a valley so dry that you don't even have the source or the principle of life - even if you wanted it." The significance of this statement lay in the philosophical teachings during this particular historical period. The understanding was that if the bones were moist, it was possible that they could be resurrected because anything that has water in it, also has life in it. But verse 2 says, that the bones were dead and lifeless.

God raises the question to the Prophet, "Son of man, can these bones live again? Because the reality is that before the reality is that before you can have a corpse with bones, there had to first be a living body. God is basically saying in verse 3, "Ezekiel, they weren't always this way; therefore, they don't have to stay this way." In other words, Ezekiel, that Brother wasn't always on drugs. That Sister, wasn't always in an abusive relationship; therefore she doesn't have to stay in an abusive relationship. That child wasn't always on the streets, therefore he can get off the streets. God was saying to Ezekiel... "Ezekiel, it doesn't have to stay that way!"

I've also heard this same question raised among the African-American Community, Can these bones live again? "Can these bones live again?" This question means that these people you see haven't always been bones.

- These people who built the first pyramid
- These people who discovered electricity.
- These people who built the first university.
- These people who unlocked the principle of mathematics.
- These people who gave you internal medicine.
- These people who gave you the first Alphabet.
- These people who plowed your fields, nursed your babies, and built your cities
- There is power in these people, so you can rightly ask, "Can these bones live again?"

Ezekiel makes a profound statement here in the text He says, "Lord, Thou knowest." Ezekiel was saying, "when I'm in trouble, I'm not going to stretch out on what I know, but I'm going to stretch out on what you know." Ezekiel was saying, "God, when I'm in trouble, I'm going to put my future in your hands." Ezekiel was saying, "O Lord God, thou knowest."

Now, I've discovered that many of us turn things over to God to escape responsibility. But what this text reminds us about resurrection ministry is this: the minute you give ultimate authority to God, get ready for an assignment. The minute that Ezekiel gave the situation over to God, then immediately God gave Ezekiel something to do. In the same way, when we turn our predicament over to God, God will always give us something to do.

God said, "Okay, Ezekiel, you're saying, 'If I know.' You're right; I do know. Now this is what I want you to do. I want you to stand up and preach my Word (v4)." God is saying, if these bones are going to live, somebody has got to stand up and preach God's Word!

Now, I have been blessed to go to school, where I have had courses in sociology and psychology. I do believe in a holistic approach to ministry, which means that if you are going to raise a people, you will need to exhaust every resource of the mind and the community, along with every other discipline at your disposal. But I also recognize that a "sociologist" can't raise bones in a valley. A psychologist can't raise folk who have reached the point where they are "scattered bones that are very dry." An urbanologist can't raise a dead people.

God doesn't say stand up and give them the latest news report about conditions in the valley. He doesn't say, stand up and lecture them on Sigmund Freud in the field of Psychology.

He doesn't say stand up and give them an analysis of urban development. Instead, He says "If my people are going to live, somebody has got to stand up and preach my Word."

If there is a contributing factor to the valley remaining full of dead people, it is because the church has preached everything but God's Word! We have preached our philosophy and our opinion. We have preached positive thinking. We've gotten our sermons from the latest statement, song, or hip-hop. We can tell them everything about this or that. We can preach rap, Oprah Winfrey, or Dr. Phil, but that can't raise a valley! Now, we may use them as illustrations to make your connection with the audience in the context of your day, but if we're going to raise a valley, we got to "stand up and preach God's Word." That's why King Zedekiah asked the prophet this question on day in Jeremiah 37:17: "Is there any word from the Lord?"

- With our country torn apart by racism, founded on racism, built and sustained by racism, is there any word from the Lord?
- With over 846,000 black men and boys in prison and privatized prisons are making billions of dollars in profits each year from housing them, is there any word from the Lord?
- With our families coming apart at the seams with 50% of every marriage in this country ending in divorce, is there any word from the Lord?
- With our Religious leaders under indictment, with our Political leaders under investigation, with our Academic leaders throwing out Affirmative Action, is there any word from the Lord?
- With 72% of African American babies born to unwed teenage mothers, is there any word from the Lord?

- With America's unemployment rate still at an all time high at 7.9% (12.3 million persons still without jobs), is there any word from the Lord?
- With the recent Emanuel AME Church massacre in Charleston South Carolina, where nine people were shot and killed, including the pastor, is there any word from the Lord?
- With Navy yard gunman Aaron Alexis going on a murderous rampage throughout Washington DC's naval base, leaving 12 people dead and at least 8 others wounded, is there any word from the Lord?
- With the recent Sandy Hook Elementary School massacre in Newtown Connecticut, where twenty children and six adult staff members were fatally shot, and as a result, now elementary school kids have to walk through metal detectors just to go to school, is there any word from the Lord?
- With the recent Supreme Court decision to support gay marriage in the United States of America, is there any word from the Lord?
- With six black churches, in five southern states targeted by arsonists or hate groups after the Charleston Nine shooting, is there any word from the Lord?
- With Sean Bell, Eric Garner, Mike Brown, John Crawford III, 12-year-old Tamir Rice and Walter Scott, all who were unarmed black men who were killed at the hands of white police officers, is there any word from the Lord?

Somebody has got to stand up and preach God's Word! Now the question becomes: What's the evidence of God's Word being preached? We might have it all wrong. In this text, when the Word was preached, nobody shouted; nobody said, "Amen," and nobody said, "Preach Ezekiel." The evidence of the Word being preached was not an invocative expression of the mouth, but an activity that happened in the Body. When the Word is truly preached folk don't say something, but they do something. What pastors want is for folks to say "Amen," but then they stay in the same condition they were in after they said, "Amen." But when the Word is truly preached, bones can't be scattered anymore. When the Word is preached we can't live in the valley anymore. When the Word is preached we can't live in the valley anymore. When the Word is preached we can't be separated anymore. When the Word is preached, we can't act like we use to act, live like we use to live, and do what we use to do – When the Word is truly preached!

Verse 7, says that there was a rattling noise. This noise was not just an expression of a response, but that of of the sound of people changing their position, identity, location, and ultimately their nature. So the evidence of preaching is not in the sound, but it's in the activity of the body. When the Word is truly preached folk don't say something, but they do something!

But this text also reminds us that it takes more than just the Word for you to be resurrected. The Word will give us "the design," but we need "the breath of God" to get our power in order to act on the design. In fact, God says, in the text God says, Ezekiel, they are in the Word. They have their form back. They are connected right. They have the right structure. They look like I want them to look. But they don't have the Power to be what I want them to be! So God tells the Prophet in times of conflict, "Prophesy (preach) to the wind."

In this verse, the Hebrew word for wind is "ruach", which means the "breath of God." God says "Now wind, I need for you to breathe on these people!" Today He says, "They have the right form. They have the choir where the choir belongs. They have the group where the group belongs. They have padded pews and padded carpet. They have a microphone/PA System. They have all the stuff in place to be a Church, but they lack one thing – "Holy Ghost Power"

But according to this text, the Word will give you the body God desires, but the Spirit will give you life, so the body can live. I like the way John Kinney, Dean of Virginia Union, says it, "Too much 'Word' and no 'Spirit', you will dry up. Too much 'Spirit' and no 'Word' you will blow up. But if you get a balance of the 'Word' and the 'Spirit', you will grow up."

But verse 4 says, God commanded Ezekiel to stand out there in that valley and preach to those dry bones. I can imagine that it was a hard Sunday, for Ezekiel. He had a hard service preaching to a congregation full of bones. Ezekiel did not have a choir to sing for him. He did not have an "Amen Corner". He did not have fiery deacons to say, "Go ahead and preach". He did not have a microphone to project his voice.

Sometimes we've got to learn how to do the job with or without. And I can see Ezekiel preaching to those bones out there in that valley. I can hear him saying, "O ye dry bones hear the Word of the Lord." And just like the Prophet said, as he preached, something started moving in that valley. He heard a noise in that valley. He heard a rumbling and a thundering in that valley. And he saw something happening that he had never seen before. He saw bones rising in the valley, and one bone was making its way to another bone.

Whatever you need is in the valley, as the song says,

"There's A Lily In The Valley"
Bright as the morning star (Repeat)
Somebody found joy in the valley
Bright as the morning star
Somebody found peace in the valley
Bright as the morning star
Somebody found love in the valley
Bright as the morning star
Somebody found hope in the valley
Bright as the morning star

Reference: Kee, John W. "The Lily in the Valley"

STRONGER IN MY BROKEN PLACES
Charles E. Booth
Exodus 32:15-20, 30-35

It would be an understatement to suggest that we live in a time when disappointments and setbacks occur on a regular basis. There has been for some time an errant theology afloat in the body of Christ that would have us belief that if we have sufficient faith we will not be victimized by disappointments, setbacks, sickness, and failures.

However, I would like to remind you of what are some of the stark realities of human existence which are applicable for saints and sinners alike. These realities are that we will experience dreadful disappointments. We will encounter shocking setbacks. We will have to deal with some toxic tension. And we will be forced to bounce back from some complicated calamities. The Bible says, the rain falls on the just and the unjust alike (see Matthew 5:45).

Anybody who lives with the notion that he or she can dodge such bullets is not living in the real world. It is for this reason that a plethora of self-help books and tapes pertaining to psychology and psychiatry are now found upon the bookcases within the average home. There are a large number of people who on a daily basis find themselves lying on a psychotherapist's couch in an attempt to deal with some heartache or heartbreak that has left them so disappointed that for them life is a very difficult pilgrimage to continue. Too many of us are ready to throw in the towel and concede to the pressures of life. People of every ethnicity are looking for assistance to make it from one day to the next.

One of the fastest-growing occupations in this culture is that of a "life coach." These individuals tend to have acquired a rudimentary understanding of psychology, theology, and sociology. People of multiple professions and various pedigrees utilize these individuals to assist them with their perpetual problems and varying situations. I have nothing against the utilization of a life coach, but I still believe that the Word of God is still "a lamp unto our feet and a light unto our path" (see Psalm 119:105). I am a firm believer that Jesus is the ultimate "Life Coach" from whom the servants of God ought to acquire their coaching. It appears that many people view Jesus as less exciting than some of the more colorful personalities we see over the airwaves today. It is no wonder that we have become such a personality and chemically dependent generation. In our insatiable need to feel attached to the ecstatic existence of this world, we are driven to seek out personalities that will allow us to live vicariously through them.

When I speak of personality dependency, I'm talking about the willingness of millions of consumers to purchase a book on the advice of a talk show host. Personality dependency occurs when you are willing to rush home from your place of employment on your limited lunch break to satisfy your daily addiction of your favorite judge from your favorite courtroom show. Personality dependency seeks to ease a disappointment or self-defined deficiency in one's life. One is truly personality dependent when they can quote a person from television more than they can recite the Bible.

When I speak of chemical dependency, I'm not simply talking about illicit drugs. I'm also talking about prescribed drugs. Some of your most chemically dependent people are those who can afford to see a medical doctor and dispense big dollars for the legally prescribed medications. So many people require medication just to function on a daily basis. How many people have a difficult time living today without antidepressants? And how many people find it very difficult to maintain a healthy relationship with anybody without the aid of chemicals?

This difficulty goes beyond the traditional relationship between a man and a woman. Some of us have a difficult time with relationships when it comes to our parents or when it comes to our siblings. There aren't many drama-free functional families or individuals in our society; however, there are a lot of functioning dysfunctional families and individuals in our society. The emotional scars from our childhood run deep into the psyche of our existence. Few of us have platonic friends primarily because the emotional and psychological scars of previous encounters and relationships have left us emotionally and psychologically broken. If a person desires to move from a state of brokenness to a posture of strength and wholeness he or she must be willing to address and deal with the brokenness from their past. Brokenness leaves a trail that can be traced for others to follow. This is why a counselor will always have you discuss your feelings about your childhood and your parents. If you want to trace your brokenness, locate your unhealed hurts, identify your unmet needs, and confess your unresolved issues. An African proverb teaches us, "A concealed disease can never be healed."

Brokenness can invade your mind, spirit, and soul at any time in your life. Brokenness can occur by way of what we hear, by way of what we see, and by way of what we experience. It would appear that many of the issues that plague our lives have their roots in our childhood. This is not to suggest that brokenness never visits us in our later years – far from it. The evidence of our societal brokenness is played out every day with the dramatic increase – among young and old, black and white, blue collar and white collar people – of this insidious disease called suicide. There are people who have decided life has become so absurd that there is nothing worthwhile left in it at all, and they would rather kill themselves than face the possibility of a troubled future. They are disappointed, disturbed, distressed, and crippled to the point that death presents a better option than life. Many people echo the sentiments of Job's pain when he said, "I curse the day of my birth. May the day of my birth perish, and the night they said, a boy is born. I wish I was never born!" (see Job 3:1-2).

There are multiple ways to address the hurt that has found residence in your soul. People deal with brokenness every day without the dependency of drugs. Black people have been dealing with the vicissitudes of life that should have annihilated us and left us broken beyond repair for years without the dependency of a human personality we thought should have been in our lives. Our women have raised strong sons and daughters, many without the assistance of a father. Our parents have worked hard and provided for their families for generations without the assistance of a just legal system. Our families have withstood the unfair practices of a people and a caste system that was hell bent on breaking our spirits, dashing our hopes, and crushing our dreams. We were not broken beyond repair then and we shall not be broken beyond repair now! How? We were able to survive because we kept our hands in the hand of the Lord. We kept our knees bent and our ears attuned to the directives of God.

One could safely make the argument that Moses should have been broken beyond repair. He was born in a country that wanted to kill him as a child; he was put in a basket upon the Nile River by his mother to escape persecution; he was raised in the household of the oppressor of his people; he was taught one thing by his mother, but exposed to another thing by the royal family during his formative years; he murdered a man when he saw the injustice against his people up close; he was forced to leave the comfort of the palace because of the information floating around town by the very people he was trying to help; he lived in the desert for forty years and then was told by God to return to a place where he ran from. Moses was broken by his desire to love a people who truly didn't love him. Moses was broken by his longing to have a greater relationship with God. Moses was broken because he suffered from a lack of self-confidence. Nevertheless, with all of these broken pieces in his life, he decided to go forward with the Lord's business.

While Moses was in the desert for forty years he underwent a metamorphosis from brokenness to wholeness. One must allow oneself to imagine the lessons that the Lord taught Moses by way of his involvement with nature, the daily farm duties of a shepherd, and the patience acquired by addressing the needs of some smelly sheep. One must allow oneself to imagine the talks Moses had with his father-in-law, Jethro, in the early dew of the morning and late into the dark nights. One must allow oneself to imagine the long walks and revealing conversations Moses shared with his wife, Zipporah.

There is something to be assumed about the movement of God's ability to insulate you after He has orchestrated the activities of your life to isolate you. Don't be afraid of going through a season of aloneness; God may be trying to help you deal with your brokenness. It is when you are in solitude that the spirit of God can adjust your attitude. Embrace your brokenness and remember that the contents of a vessel can't be utilized until the seal has been broken.

Since life can render us disappointing times, since life presents to us setbacks, what then can we do as God's servants in moving from brokenness to wholeness? What is that which can be lifted from the life of Moses that can help us deal and cope with the challenges of life? How can God use us as He heals us? Moses displays three things we can do to help us move from our brokenness to wholeness.

The first thing the text suggests we do to become stronger is to be willing to serve as an intercessor between God and His people. Learning that the people had committed the dastardly sin of making themselves gods, Moses knew he had to serve as a go-between to help the people restore their covenantal relationship with God. Moses knew he had to help the people keep their eyes fixed upon the God of all creation and deliverance. Moses was broken when the Lord instructed him, "Go down, because your people, whom you brought up out of Egypt, have become corrupt" (see Exodus 32:7).

Many times we become broken because of the things that we hear from God. Moses was broken because he had to break his communion with the Lord because of the actions of other people. Too often we allow the actions of others to break our communion with God. As Moses departed from the top of the mountain one can only imagine what was going through his psyche. Moses had to wonder how a people could willingly defy such a gracious God. Moses knows he will have to serve as God's spokesman and assist them in their understanding of who God actually is and what God has actually done for the people of Israel. It bothered him that the newly freed people, who had just recently agreed to keep the covenant with the Lord, quickly forgot who brought them out of bondage.

How many of us are living in the midst of our brokenness because we decided to move away from God by breaking our personal agreements with God? Many people today aren't willing to have someone serve as an intercessor for them. However, as an intercessor, one must be willing to declare to the people what thus says the Lord.

In today's society many people need a liaison to remind them who can deliver them from their brokenness and make them stronger from their experience. Many people insist on pushing their harsh realities underneath the proverbial rug of denial. Someone needs to serve as a third party between a person's pain and God's graciousness. One is not so spiritually self-sufficient that one doesn't need the assistance of others. None of us have it so all together that disappointments don't rock us sometimes and make us feel and wonder if we have a friend in heaven or on the earth. It is imperative for us to admit that sometimes we need to be reassured of the reality that there is a mighty God who sits high but looks low. God has gifted humanity with people in all walks of life to help us understand the mysteries of their existence.

Medical people in the world of anatomy and physiology teach and tell us that whenever a bone is broken and is properly set, its healing will allow the point of the break to be stronger than before. Please don't miss the truth of this anatomical illustration. The strongest point in your body is that place where you have experienced brokenness and God has allowed through the miracle of medicine and the miracle of His touch to heal and restore your breakage. Anybody who has broken an arm, broken a wrist, broken a leg, or broken an ankle can attest to the fact that at the healing point of the breakage emerged a greater strength. Therefore, a broken heart today has the potential to be a stronger heart tomorrow. A damaged mind today has the opportunity to be a stronger mind tomorrow. A bruised self-image today has the resiliency to become a stronger self-image tomorrow. A dysfunctional person today has the opportunity to become a functional person tomorrow. We are stronger in our broken places.

If this be true of the human body, if this is an anatomical and physiological axiom, then it must also be true spiritually. At the place I break, if I allow the Holy Spirit to reset the breakage, I don't have to fall apart at the seams. I don't have to go around as if I'm somebody without hope because the point where I am broken – if I allow God to heal the wound – becomes the point of my strength. We are stronger in our broken places.

The church ought to be a place where the broken have a chance to be made whole. All too often a person who claims to be a Christian gives God a black eye and the church a bad name because he or she doesn't know how to handle his or her breakage. As we see here in the text many of the people had a difficult time waiting on Moses to return from the Lord. Many people like to regress to some of their old habits to help them deal with their brokenness. You don't have to handle your brokenness with drugs, alcohol, or with sexual promiscuity. I understand everyone falls short of the glory of God, but as a Christian one ought to acknowledge that God strengthened you at the point of your brokenness. Your brokenness becomes your testimony. Your brokenness becomes your credential that allows you to encourage someone else of God's power and might.

Moses had to address his brokenness based on what he heard from God before he could adequately address the brokenness of the people. Although broken by the behavior of the people, Moses understood that he had to allow God to use him to get the people back on course with God and in alignment with the will of God. He understood the people had to learn how to wait and trust the movement of God. Moses understood that a mangled people today have the power, with the grace of God, to become a stronger people tomorrow.

Moses is broken because of what he heard from God, but he becomes even more broken because of what he sees the people actually doing. He sees a people who have truly disrespected their God and committed a deadly sin. Moses loses it and he breaks the tablets. He smashes them on the ground. Then he looks at the idol and throws it into the fire. He grinds the powder from the ashes, sprinkles it in the water, and instructs the people to drink their own ideology. Moses is really disappointed by their act of debauchery and immorality. Nevertheless, he understands that despite his feelings he must allow himself to edify the people. One way God helps us transition from our broken state is by using us to assist others in their brokenness. We all must learn to deal with our hurt while seeking to help others. One cannot give up or give in to their pain and disappointments while attempting to enlighten others.

The second thing that Moses teaches is we should define ourselves more by our disappointments than by our dreams. More strength came forth from Moses' disappointments than from his dreams. The same is the case for us. The reason that I come to this is because, in most instances, one has more disappointments in life than dreams. Some of our dreams are on hold. Some of our dreams will never materialize. We are defined more by our disappointments than we are by our dreams. It is in the trials of life that authentic character gets a chance to reveal itself.

It was never the dream of Moses to become Israel's liberator. It was never the dream of Moses to go before Pharaoh and challenge his rule. His dream was to become a prince and remain in all of grandeur that Egypt had to offer him as an Egyptian prince. That was Moses' dream. But that wasn't God's dream. God can be annoying by quietly converting our dreams and allowing us to live within what appears to be disappointing situations in order to bring His plan to pass in our lives.

Jochebed, Moses' mother, had been taken to Pharaoh's daughter by Miriam. It was Jochebed who actually nursed Moses, and she nurses him by reciting in his hearing the history of his people. One day at 40 years old, Moses goes to Goshen, which is the Jewish ghetto, and he witnesses an Egyptian beating a Hebrew. He can't take it. His rage rises, violence takes over, and he kills the Egyptian and buries his body in the sand. He becomes a murderer. He never dreamed of becoming that. Then he runs and he becomes a fugitive from justice. And for the next forty years of his life, he lives in the desert of Midian. He meets Jethro, the priest, who becomes his father-in-law and his counselor. He marries and has children. So now he's living out in the desert – that's a long way from the palace. Some may define his life as disappointed. One thing is for sure – it wasn't a part of his dream for his life.

Then God calls him. Now God can be annoying. I mean, God is the kind of deity who will add insult to injury. Moses is not a prince anymore. He's living out in the desert. He's married, has all these kids, and then God says, "I want you to go back and inform Pharaoh that I'm going to pull the rug out from under his economy and take the slave population and lead them into the land of promise."

Moses is not molded by his dreams. Moses is molded by his disappointments. For the young and old alike who are trying to put their lives back together again because of some dream that has yet to come true, stay strong in the Lord. Accept that when the Lord allows disappointment to happen, it means there's something in the disappointment that He is trying to get you to see. Disappointment must be redefined when looked at through the lenses of God.

Some of you have been looking at this thing totally wrong. You want to look at every disappointment as being from the Devil. You want to think that every setback comes from the adversary. No. Some of this stuff comes from God. I know you don't want to believe it, but God will sometimes make you go through hell to really appreciate Him. Sometimes He'll make you cry so that you can really laugh about something. How can you appreciate the mountain if you haven't walked through the valley? How can you appreciate the sunshine if you haven't been in the rain and in the clouds? Disappointments ultimately are not millstones; they are stepping stones.

You must learn how to recycle disappointment. You must be willing to grapple with the issues of life and learn to depend on God for guidance through your rough times. Disappointments can help you develop your devotional time with God. It can help you develop purposeful prayer life. It is in your disappointments that you are encouraged to develop a more consistent Bible study ritual. You're not defined by your dreams; you are defined by your disappointments. As Booker T. Washington said, "Success is not measured by the position one has reached in life, rather the obstacles overcome while trying to succeed."

I have always been enraptured with Alex Haley's Roots – not just with Roots, but with the sequel Roots: The Next Generation. What a marvelous story of one man's family. The story of Alex Haley's family is your story and mine. All of the authenticity of our inner strength can be traced back to Kunta Kinte. Look at the story and how he was brought to this country after being snatched out of a Gambian jungle while going out to look for wood in order to make something. The dream was that he would be forever successful in that village. But he was captured by slave traders, taken across the watery deep of the Atlantic, survived the Middle Passage, and brought here to this land called America, where they cut off his foot and finally succeeded to change his name from Kunta Kinte to Toby.

Roots is the story of a lineage that defines disappointment in the context of stepping stones and not millstones. Alex Haley tried to live in his father's dream. However, he was unsuccessful in his efforts. Many people are living challenging lives trying to live their parents' dream. God never told you to live their dream. You have to live your own dreams.

Simon Haley wanted Alex to be a college graduate, but Alex wanted to be a writer. He dropped out of college and joined the Coast Guard. While in the Coast Guard, against his father's wishes, he married and had children. The marriage fell apart and he and his wife divorced, but he kept pursuing his own dream. He writes The Autobiography of Malcolm X with Malcolm X. He writes to his father on the inside of an autographed copy, "I no longer need your approval, but I'll always need your love." He goes on to write Roots and to become one of the most prolific writers in our generation. He would have never become that if he had viewed his disappointments as a millstone. He became stronger in his place of brokenness. He's stronger because he understood that his disappointments made him the person who he was meant to be at the insistence of God.

Who does God want you to be? Are you willing to accept the plans of God for your life as He reveals them to you? Saul of Tarsus wanted to be a great rabbi like Gamaliel, but that isn't who God wanted him to be. God wanted him to become Paul the Apostle to the Gentiles in Asia Minor.

Nelson Mandela wanted to be a lawyer, but God had another plan. He wanted him to be locked up for twenty-seven years, so that he could eventually become the first Black president of South Africa.

Martin Luther King, Jr. had a dream of succeeding Benjamin Mays as the President of Morehouse College. That was his dream. God had another dream for him – to be our Black Moses who would go up against segregation and discrimination.

Who does God want you to be? Maybe you're struggling in your life because you have not properly defined your disappointment. Are still kicking trying to live out a dream that God never intended for you?

Moses dreamed of becoming a prince, but God meant for him to become a liberator. Moses dreamed of giving instructions to slaves, as a prince, but God wanted him to become an instructor of the slaves, as a prophet. It did not matter that he was raised in Egyptian culture. It did not matter that he spoke Hebrew with an Egyptian accent. It did not matter that he was even a murderer. Disappointments afforded Moses the opportunity to develop an outer shell of tough skin and an inner layer of assurance of God's power.

Moses teaches us that our disappointments help make us the people who God means for us to be, and not the person we dream of becoming. Whatever your hurts, whatever your pains, whatever your setbacks, and whatever your disappointments, they can never take away the last of your human freedoms as you move from brokenness to wholeness.

The final thing that Moses teaches us to do as we move from our brokenness to our strength is to exercise our right to choose what our attitude will be in any given circumstance. Moses says to the people, "You have committed a great sin. But now I will go up to the Lord; perhaps I can make atonement for you sins." It doesn't matter what has happened to you; you still have an option of the attitude you will have towards that incident. You are free to respond to the pain as you choose to do so. Typically, people respond to their brokenness in one of two ways. You can either let the pain control you or you can control the pain. In either case, you've got to make an attitude adjustment. You have to learn how to roll with the punches of life, and display an attitude of a victor and not that of a victim. Benjamin Mays once said, "To be able to stand the troubles of life, one must have a sense of mission and a belief that God sent him or her into the world for a purpose, to do something unique and distinctive; and if he or she does not do it, life will be worse off because it was not done."

All of us must make the conscious decision to succeed in life by making the decision not to fail in life. One can either allow their peril to break them or build them. In the end, it is imperative for all us to take the responsibility for our own destiny as we rely on the activities of God in our lives. When travail visits you and you start to feel gloomy, step back and encourage yourself by acknowledging that you need an attitude adjustment.

In a heavyweight championship fight between the champ Mike Tyson and a little-known fighter name Buster Douglas a few years ago, Buster was knocked down and it appeared that Iron Mike had assaulted another victim in the boxing ring. However, on this day Buster Douglas was fighting for more than a title belt. He was fighting for the pride and honor of his recently deceased mother. His strength was both physical and spiritual. In the deepest corridors of his existence was the battle cry of his mother, "You can do it." Buster had to choose to stay down or get up. Not only did he get up, he went on to knock out the supposedly invincible heavyweight champion of the world.

Moses had a choice: stay mad and angry or adopt the nature of his Creator. Too many people allow themselves to stay down on the canvas of life. Moses had in the desert forty years with people who probably taught him how to appreciate life for what it is and not for what he felt it should have been. It is plausible that Jethro, his father-in-law, could have taught him another side of God that was slightly different from his Egyptian rearing. God still has good folk in many places who can help you learn things about God that will enhance your attitude towards Him and your views toward your disappointments. God still has open doors that no man can shut. Don't allow yourself to be surrounded with people who specialize in toxic testimonies of the mundane. They are poisoning your attitude. You have to surround yourself with some people who can feed you a healthy dose of "you can make it" affirmations. You have to believe that you can rise above whatever or whoever is trying to break you.

Moses could have stayed angry; he could have stayed bitter. But instead he decides to adopt the nature of his Creator. He goes to God and dialectally he presents a thesis: "Now Lord, if you have to blot out anybody, blot me out. The people have sinned. There isn't any doubt about that. But I want mercy for the people. When I look back over my life, I see is empathy, I see compassion, I see grace. It started out when I was born, when Pharaoh was committing genocide and killing all Hebrew male children. I survived the Nile and ended up in the enemy's bathing pool, and the oppressor had to raise the liberator. Then I killed that Egyptian one day and buried his body in the sand. But you gave me another chance – grace. So I want you to forgive their sin. They're wrong. They should have never fashioned the image of the golden calf. They should have never gotten involved in debauchery and immorality. But if you can put it on me and let them live, that will be all right."

But God says, "That's all right. I hear what you're saying. But they are going to pay for what they did." In my spiritual imagination I can hear God telling Moses, "What they did was not an affront to you, but to me. But I'll tell you what, my servant, although you can't atone for their sin, I will allow you to be an ambassador and lead them to the promised land of milk and honey because you have made an attitude adjustment towards the people. And Moses, relax, I already have Somebody who's waiting in the wings of time who will be a suitable atonement for the sin of people. It isn't His time yet. One day, in the fullness of time, I'm going to send my Son, who's going to tiptoe down the stairway of heaven to atone for sin." It is imperative to know that Moses was not an acceptable atonement for the people of Israel. However, he was an acceptable vessel to serve as liberator for the people of Israel on behalf of God.

Moses could have chosen to stay in his brokenness, but he was willing to serve as an intercessor between God and His people. More strength came forth from Moses' disappointments than from his dreams. He chose what his attitude would be in many circumstances. As in the time of Moses, we live in a time when disappointments and setbacks occur on a regular basis, but like Moses, we are stronger in our broken places. Now that you have come to the end of this book, I want to encourage you to shout: I am stronger in my broken places!

How To Survive With Seven Skinny Cows When The Economy Is Shot
James C. Perkins
Genesis 41: 1-36

Within the unlimited boundaries of His wide wonderful providence, our Father God has always made adequate provisions for His children. No matter what there is in our lives that we may have to complain about, no reasonable person can uncover any scandal, or produce any evidence worthy of filing a paternity suit against God and accusing Him of non-support.

God is not like some of us in that He did not produce a world full of babies and retreat to some remote corner of the universe shirking His duty and responsibility. He has not created false hope within us. He has not created obligations for Himself that He has not more than adequately fulfilled.

From the beginning of the human project, God demonstrated His concern for our well being by providing for the care and welfare of all His creatures. He made the stately trees to provide shelter for the birds before He created the birds. And though times get tough and the going gets rough, I've never seen a bird holding up a sign that reads, "Will chirp for food." He made the rocky caverns to house the beasts of the field before He made the beasts. And no matter how rough and tough the times may be, I've yet to see even a junkyard dog needing to spend a night or two in a homeless shelter.

Whatever our vast and varied opinions of God may be, we certainly cannot accuse Him of non-support. He is a wonderful Father who takes care of His own. He has not promised to make us rich, or to transport us through life on flowery beds of ease. But He has promised to take care of us and to supply all of our needs. And that He has and that He does is a fact of life that none of us can dispute or deny.

There is a very real danger in the course of our living of losing sight of the fact that it is God who takes care of us. We have this self-centered tendency to get so carried away with ourselves that we are prone to forget that without God, we can do nothing!

Without God, we wouldn't enjoy the measure of health and strength we are privileged to enjoy. Without God, We wouldn't have the job to work that we do have. Without God, we wouldn't have any pennies to pull together to make it as well as we are. Without God, we can do nothing.

We have become so obsessed with the notion that we have got to make it for ourselves that we forget that it is the Lord who makes a way for us. We have become so preoccupied with trying to meet our bread and butter needs that we forget that we do no live by bread alone. For some reason, we don't seem to accept the fact that it is God who enables us to make it.

We don't mind trusting God when it comes to the intangible issues of life over which we have no control. We will gladly call Him "a doctor who haws never lost a patient" when we get sick. We willingly see Him as a lawyer in the courtroom when we get in trouble. We willingly see Him as a heart fixer and a mind regulator when we get stressed out and upset. We willingly see Him as a Savior from our sins when we are haunted by our moral failure.

Our religious conditioning has mainly taught us to see God as a God who is concerned about our misery, but not our money. We see Him as a God who is concerned about our emotions, but not our economics. We see God as a God that we call on to deliver us from our misery and our mess, but not a God who is concerned about social justice, economic exploitation, and how we treat other people.

And that is bad, my brothers and sisters. That is bad because God is not just in the business of delivering us from our mess. He is a God who seeks to be the primary focus of our lives. He wants us to worship Him. He wants us to put Him first. He wants us to align our lives with His Word and His will. He wants us to make Him the Head of our lives.

We are living and we are worshipping in a spiritual atmosphere where there is an imbalance in our theology. We have a one-eyed theology.

- We are being conditioned to see God as a god who gives.
- We see God as a god who blesses.
- We see God as a god who looks beyond our faults and sees our need.

But we are failing to see God as a God who judges, who calls us to accountability, and who will punish us for our misdeeds.

We have a one-sided view of God. We don't like to see Him as a God who curses; who judges us for our sin; and who punishes us for our disobedience. We don't like this side of God. We don't like it because it doesn't suit our purpose. It doesn't conform to our personal agendas. We want to bling bling. We want to be a little spiritual "show stopper." We want to be a little celebrity Christian – preacher and not a true gospel prophet.

We don't like the "tough love" streak in God that causes Him to put us in our place when we get out of line. We don't like this side of God. This is why we think we can do anything we want to do and still be blessed. You are not going to be blessed anyhow.

This is why, when Jeremiah Wright says, "God will damn America for its racism, its social injustice, and the economic exploitation of its people," people who have a one-eyed theology wanted to crucify him. A one-eyed theology is theology of a one-eyed god. And we don't have a one-eyed god. Our God sees everything. The old preacher used to say, "He sits high, but He looks low."

He sees the issue, but He sees beneath the surface of the issue. He sees all the maneuverings that co-mingled to create the issue.

A one-eyed god sees things your way, but we serve a God who is omniscient. He sees everything. He sees everybody, and He sees everywhere! Nothing sneaks up on Him. Nothing and nobody can blindside Him. He sees everything.

He sees the good and the bad not just of individuals, but also of nations. He sees the evil machinations of individuals and of nations.

Our God sees everything! You better mind how you walk. You better mind how you talk. You better mind how you treat other people. You better check yourself before you wreck yourself. Our God sees everything!

He is not just a God who blesses. He is also a God who judges. He judges individuals, and He judges nations. There is a very real sense in which it can be said that at this tick of the watch in history, our nation is under judgment because we have mis-represented God.

We claim to be a God loving and a God fearing nation. But the truth is that for all of our history, we have mis-represented God. We have made God appear to be a god who is on the side of the strong, the wealthy, and the powerful.

And in His name, we have stepped on the weak, stepped over the poor, and accused the powerless of being lazy and irresponsible. We have blamed the weak, the powerless, and the poor for not only being in the condition they're in, but for all that's gone wrong in the world.

The weak, the powerless, and the poor are being blamed for the collapse of the economy. The weak, the powerless, and poor are being blamed for the housing crisis. The weak, the powerless, and the poor are blamed for the deterioration of the public school system.

And after a certain point, God has grown tired of it and is registering His discontent. Even in our religion we have misrepresented God. Our religion is rooted more in American capitalism than it is in biblical faith.

A whole lot of preachers are preaching that the essence of the gospel is personal prosperity; "bling bling" and not economic justice. We want a life that's blessing full and trouble free. And as a result, we don't mind trying to P-I-M-P God. We will grudgingly throw a few pennies His way some time if He'll make us look good all the time.

We've tried to turn God into a platinum God, a worthless golden calf. Even in our religion we are selfish and greedy. We want everything for us and we won't help anybody.

We have all of these denominations: AME, AMEZ, CME, ABC, NBC, PNBC, etc. We've got mega churches in minor neighborhoods, and despite all of that, collectively we don't even have a pot to cook a chicken in!

God has put the nation under judgment. God says, "Ok, you bad! I tell you what I'm going to do. I'm going to put you in a seven skinny cow situation and then see what you do."

In the background of this text, God is about to judge Egypt. He is about to judge them because they're oppressing His people. Egypt has reached the zenith of its power. They are feeling as smug as a bug in a rug. They're feeling secure and impregnable. Pharaoh is feeling His oats. He is feeling the opulence and omnipotence of empire.

And God says, "I've got to send them a message to let them know who's in charge."

Pharaoh went to bed as usual that night. He fell asleep as usual that night. And as soon as he was sleeping soundly and comfortably, God sent him a telepathic psycho-spiritual message. That's what a dream is. It is divine telepathy. It is a psycho-spiritual message that God inserts into the database of our soul.

Pharaoh dreamed. And in his dream, he saw the plush and lush pastoral landscape surrounding the Nile River. He saw himself standing by its fertile banks when suddenly there emerged up out of its liquid bosom seven fat healthy cows that grazed among the reeds.

Such a comforting image. Pharaoh snuggled between his 900 thread Egyptian cotton sheets. Then suddenly there emerged again from the waters of the Nile, seven skinny cows. They seemed so weak they could hardly stand. They had a lean and hungry look. When they looked around, they saw these seven fat healthy cows and ate up the seven fat healthy cows. Pharaoh's spirit was shocked. He woke up disturbed.

You've had that experience before, haven't you? You have had dreams where God awakens you, and you break out in a cold sweat, all upset, disturbed, and unable to go back to sleep. It has you shaking and sitting on the side of the bed scratching your head trying to figure out the meaning of the dream.

Pharaoh was disturbed. He lay back down and dreamed the same dream again only this time with seven ears of corn. Cows and corn: the staples of their economy. In that day, a person's standard of living was determined by whether they had enough corn to feed the number of cows they had.

Now notice that he went to sleep. He woke up. And then he went back to sleep again. And, as it turns out, he was disturbed by what occurred in his dream.

This nation has done terrible things. I don't see how Bush and Cheney and that Tea Party crew could sleep at night! The innocent lives taken. The countries destroyed! Saddam was murdered on TV like a reality show. Look at the havoc they have reeked with the economy.

They can walk around all arrogant and proud and forget, but God is not going to forget. The late Dr. D. E. King used to say, "If God doesn't destroy America, He owes Sodom and Gomorrah an apology."

Some people can do anything and sleep just fine. You may not want to believe it, but there are folks who could stab you in the back and sleep just fine! Everybody ain't happy for you!

Pharaoh woke up a second time. It wasn't the fat cows grazing in the grass that upset him. That was the restful and snuggly part of the dream. As long as he was looking at those seven fat cows grazing in the meadow, he stretched out and got more comfortable.

No, it was not the fat cows. It was the seven skinny cows. They looked bad. They were ugly. And on top of that they turned around and ate up the seven fat healthy cows. That was unnatural. That was shocking. That was disturbing.

Pharaoh called in all of his experts. The soothsayers. The wizards. The magicians. All who were supposed to have the knowledge and ability to interpret his dream. He told them the dream, but none of them could interpret it.

Isn't that the predicament we find ourselves in today? All the experts have failed. We wanted Barack to be a magician. After the awful hand he was dealt, they say he had three years. They would not pass any programs he submitted to Congress; yet he kept the country from complete financial collapse and ruin.

The so-called prophets have failed. The economists have failed. The legislators have failed. All the experts have failed. Nobody from Harvard, Yale, Stanford, U-MI, or any institution of higher learning knows what to do. Nobody saw it coming, and nobody knows what to do to get us out of it.

The experts have failed because they see and plan a future that is inconsistent with the future God sees and wants for us. He has to use something simple, but complex to confound them. What is simpler than a dream? What is more common than a dream? Simple, common, but complex. Everyone dreams, but only God can give the interpretation.

Pharaoh's experts failed him. His cupbearer got over his amnesia and suddenly remembered that when he was in prison, a Hebrew boy had interpreted his dream. He told Pharaoh about Joseph. Pharaoh sent for Joseph. And Joseph told him the meaning of his dream. He said these seven skinny cows represented seven years of famine and of economic hardship.

My brothers and sisters, that's where we are today. We are in a seven skinny cow situation. (The city is bankrupt) I hate to tell you, but the fat cow days are over. The economy is shot. Everything and everybody is skinnying down.

Notice these cows. They were skinny. This suggest that they were under-nourished and under-fed. There are a whole lot of people who are under-nourished, under-fed, under-housed, under-employed and because the policies of this nation have put them in this situation. God uses seven Skinny Cow times to call attention to the underserved portion of the population. Pharaoh can starve po' Black folk, but God can starve a Pharaoh.

Notice the skinny cows' actions. They turned and ate up the seven fat cows. This was their survival strategy. Skinny cow times threaten your standard of living.

You're used to being fat! You're used to living large! Before these times, your standard of living was about the level of seven fat cows. Now all of what you've accumulated is being threatened.

Notice that there were seven. This is the degree of the severity of the famine. On a scale of 1 to 7 the Great Depression was just about a three skinny cow famine. Wall Street would be glad if this was about a five skinny cow famine. But this is a seven skinny cow situation.

But it doesn't matter how severe it is. The good news is that God can get you out of it. It doesn't matter if the economy is shot, God will still take care of you. It doesn't matter how pervasive and endless it seems, God has a strategy. This text teaches us how to survive a seven Skinny Cow economic melt down.

I. Focus On God, Don't Focus On The Situation

Joseph said, "It is not in me. God will give Pharaoh an answer of peace." Seven skinny cow times make you nervous. Some of us have already lost our houses. Some of us have already lost our jobs. And all of us are feeling a little insecure. We literally don't know what to expect next.

This condition is so unprecedented and so pervasive that we don't know where to look for help. In the ordinary crises of our lives we could turn to family; turn to the credit union, or draw something out of one those fat cow accounts you had on the side. But now things are so tight, there's nowhere to run, and nobody to run to. We're being threatened and devoured by these seven skinny cow times, and the temptation is to so focus on our circumstance that we forget about God.

My brothers and sisters, don't become so consumed about how bad things are that you lose sight of the fact that in good times and bad times, God is still good! God is still able! God is in charge! God knows where you are. God knows what you're going through. And He knows how you're going to turn out.

Pharaoh wanted to focus on the circumstance. "What does this mean? You've got to tell me. This has me upset. Nobody knows what to do." But Joseph said, "The answer ain't in me. It's in God." And the answer is in God! The answer ain't in Barack. The answer is in "The Rock"! The answer ain't in the government. The answer is in the Savior! Don't hook your hope to false deliverers. The answer is in God. It doesn't matter who's in the White House, God is still on the Throne!

Looking at the circumstance and getting all upset about how bad things look won't do anything but make you feel worse. But lift up your eyes unto the hills from whence your help comes. The Lord is my Shepherd. The Lord is my light and my salvation.

Focus on God. It'll make you feel better. It will fill you full of hope. You can use this situation to straighten some things out between you and God. The truth be told when you were strutting around here like you were so fat, you were skinny acting towards God's causes.

Sometimes God can't get your attention. When you thought of yourself as being fat, you tried to starve God's causes. Now that you are skinny and your fat status is threatened, you can use this time to tell God you're sorry. I'm sorry. Will you feed me? Will you give me some money? Will you forgive me?

Joseph caused Pharaoh to shift his focus from circumstance to God. Pharaoh was looking at the circumstance. He was anxious that there was going to be a famine in his land. He said to Joseph, "You can tell me what to do?" Joseph replied, "The answer is not in me, but in God. He will give you an answer of peace."

Focus on God. He will give you answer of peace. Peace is what you need in a seven skinny cow time. Focusing on the circumstance will make you nervous, anxious, and worried. It will send shivers up and down your spine. But God will give you peace. Focus on God, not on the circumstance. The circumstance is bad, but God is still good!

Circumstances change, but God is the same yesterday, today and forevermore. The circumstance may be tough, but God is God over the circumstance. Focus on God. Papa said He's water in a dry place and He's bread in a starving land. He's food on your table. He's a roof over your head.

Focus on God. Serve Him. Declare His goodness! Be faithful to Him even and especially in a seven skinny cow time. He will never leave you nor forsake you.

I've been around here long enough now to have seen some tnings. I've seen some things. I've seen the mighty fall from positions of power and influence. I've seen men launch a rocket and land on the moon. I've seen hard times and bad times before. "I once was young, but now I'm old, but I've never seen the righteous forsaken, or His seed begging bread." (Psalm 37:25)

I have never seen a praying man's prayer go unanswered. I have never seen God break His promise! And He promised never to leave me, Never to leave me alone. He'll feed you. He'll provide for you. He'll take care of you. He'll make a way for you even in a seven skinny cow time.

Focus on God. Don't focus on the circumstance.

II. Think "Us" And Not "I"

In Pharaoh's dream, the seven skinny cows turned on and ate up the seven fat cows. This was their survival strategy. They were thinking "I." In skinny times, you can't help but think about yourself. In fact, you become preoccupied with the "I." How am "I" going to make it? What am "I" going to do? How am "I" going to take care of my family? The temptation is to get jealous of other folks because in spite of the skinny times, they still look fat; like they're doing pretty good while you're struggling!

The fact is we got in this situation by thinking "I." When we thought of ourselves as being more secure, more stable, a little fatter than we are now, we thought "I." We looked down in derision and scorn on people who weren't doing as well as we were. Our attitude was, and still is, "I" got mine. You get yours! It doesn't take much for us to think "I," But the way to survive this skinny cow time is not by turning on each other.

These seven skinny cows did eat up the seven fat cows, but it didn't help them any. After they finished eating them up, they were still skinny cows. Some folks' way of surviving is by taking what you've got. I had a man tell me, "I ain't going down by myself Rev. If I go down, I'm taking somebody with me." You know, misery loves company!

No. No. The way to survive is not by thinking "I," but by thinking "us." That's how our foreparents made it through the skinny times. You see, we are nervous. We are anxious. We don't know what to do because most of us have never seen hard times and skinny times before. But ours is a history of survival through skinny times. How did we go from picking cotton to picking presidents? Because our foreparents thought "us," not "I."

We say, "I got mine. You get yours." They said, "If I've got something, you've got something." We say, "What's mine is mine." They said, "Just call on me brother, if you need a hand. We all need somebody to lean on." They thought "us," not "I."

If they ran out of salt and pepper, they could send next door and borrow some from Mary because they thought "us", not "I."They would have church services and pool their pennies, and nickels, and dimes to help send each other's children to go to school because they thought "us," not "I."

Pharaoh woke from his dream at the point where the seven skinny cows ate up the seven fat cows because they didn't improve themselves. We are not going to improve ourselves by turning on each other and being jealous of each other and wanting somebody to do bad because you're doing bad.

The way to survive is by turning to each other and everyone looks out for each other by bringing your share to the storehouse. That's what Joseph suggested. He said, "Pharaoh, you can't have your people turning on each other. Tell them to put up a fifth of everything in the storehouse. And when they get hungry, they can come to the storehouse."That's what our foreparents did. They filled up the storehouse. And when anybody needed anything, they came to the storehouse.

But "us?" We're so consumed with "I" that we have neglected the storehouse. We're so selfish and greedy, we don't care if the storehouse gets shutdown.

God is calling us in this crisis to get together. This crisis requires an African communal response and not the European approach of rugged individualism. You can't make it by yourself. You aren't big enough. You aren't bad enough. You don't have enough. You won't be around long enough. We all need the storehouse.

They filled up the storehouse. And every time somebody needed something, they came to the storehouse. The last time I checked, the church is the storehouse. "Bring ye all the tithes into the storehouse that there may be meat in my house." (Malachi 3:10)

Bread is in the storehouse. Water is in the storehouse. Hope is in the storehouse. Joy in my House. Encouragement in my House. Determination in my House. Perseverance in my House.

Think "us" and not "I!"

III. It Doesn't Come To Stay

Joseph was quick to point out that this famine was going to last for seven years. Seven in the scriptures represents completeness, total, pervasive. And this famine was all over the world as it is this day, but it was to last for only seven years.

Seven years is not a long time, but it is long enough when it is a seven skinny cow time. The only redeeming feature is that it has a definite beginning and a definite end - seven years.

In a seven skinny cow time, you scratch for everything you get. In a seven skinny cow time, you can't afford the luxuries, only the necessities. In a seven skinny cow time, you wonder sometimes where your next meal is coming from.

Seven years is not a long time, but it is long enough when it is skinny cow time. God sends these times to get our attention. He wants to remind us who's in charge. And He wants us to know that in fat times or skinny times, He is God and there is no other besides Him.

He knows that in fat times some of us are skinny acting towards His storehouse and towards His causes. And He wants to let us know that He can starve us all out. If you don't serve Him, if you don't honor Him, if you don't put Him first, He can put you out of business. If you don't treat other people right, He can shut you down.

Seven years is not a long time, but it is long enough for God to make His point. Most of all He wants you to know that He will not fail you. He is still Jehovah Jirah even in the skinny times. He will take care of us. It might seem like you're never going to get through this, but hang on in there, because it's not going to last.

Weeping may endure for a night, but it doesn't last. Joy comes in the morning. He will still put food on your table. He will still pay the mortgage every month. He will still provide your every need according to His riches in glory.

Be not dismayed whate'er betide
God will take care of you
Beneath His wings of love abide
God will take care of you

In lean times, He'll take care of you. In tough times, He'll take care of you. It's a mean time! It's a lean time! It's a skinny, skinny, skinny cow time! It's a rough time! It's a tough time! It's a help me, help me Lord time! But I know that He will supply all our needs according to his riches up in glory!

ON BREAKING THROUGH BARRIERS
Raphael G. Warnock
Mark 16: 1-8

When Jesus came, He came breaking through and breaking down barriers. He came letting in those who were locked out. Jesus cracked every glass ceiling, opened the gate, and gave us all access to God.

In a very real sense, that was His mission, His ministry, and in a very real sense, that was His mission, His ministry, and the meaning of His message. Put another way, he is both Redeemer and Liberator. As Redeemer, He embraces us. As Liberator, He emancipates us. We know that He is the Redeemer, "For God so loved the world that He gave His only begotten son that whosoever believeth on him…" And we know that He is the Liberator for He came preaching "deliverance to the captives," and "the one whom the Son sets free is free indeed." He is the believers' barrier breaker.

He breaks through the barriers of class. The poor hear good news. The workday lives of ordinary fishermen, like Andrew and Simon, James and John, the sons of Zebedee are interrupted to do extraordinary work. "Follow me." He breaks through spiritual barriers. Demoniacs are delivered. He breaks through religious and cultural barriers. Lepers who have been quarantined because of sickness and the social stigma associated with their sickness are cleansed and included again in the community.

And He breaks through the barriers of gender. Women are among His disciples. They play a major role in His Galilean ministry. Mary Magdalene and Mary, the mother of James, and Salome are all disciples of Jesus. Make no mistake about it. They, too, are His disciples. In fact, they all follow Him and finance His ministry. Mark 15.41 says "These used to follow him and provided for him when he was in Galilee; and there were many other women who had come up with him to Jerusalem." Like every other preacher I know, where in the world would Jesus be were it not for the women?

Well, it's Sunday morning and whom do we encounter again? The women! They are the last at the cross and the first at the tomb. The text tells that it is very early. The sun had risen. They do not know that the Son had risen. And so, they come not out of a sense of expectation but dedication. They've come out of a sense of devotion and love for the One who loved them and lifted and liberated them and gave them new life. They've come to embalm His body. They've come to the tomb looking for Jesus so that they might see Him and serve Him one more time. Just one more time! If they could but touch Him, who had touched them! They want to get to Jesus!

I wonder if there is anybody reading this sermon who wants to get to Jesus? I mean you desperately need to get to another place in your life. You don't go to church to show out or to show off, to see or to be seen. But you go to church because you're tired of being stuck and you're not content where you are. I don't know about you but I need to get to Jesus!

They want to get to Him but there is something in their way. The end of the preceding chapter tells us that a large stone had been rolled against the door of the tomb. It says that Joseph of Arimathea rolled it there. But a stone like this was be very large and very heavy, and Joseph, a member of elite society, no doubt had several hired men to do what no one man could do. Several men were needed to put this stone in place. And, three brave and determined women have come to do what would have taken several men to accomplish. Sometimes we sincerely and desperately want to get to God, but there is something or someone or some issue in our way. Don't let anything or anyone stop you!

What is in your way, blocking your ability to get closer to Jesus? The good news is that He wants to get close to you. No matter your past, you can get close to God. As a matter of fact, God is not far from anyone of us. "For in Him, we live…" Mary Magdalene understood that. For out of her, He cast seven demons. Mary, the mother of James, could testify. She had been with Him through rejection and persecution and the ups and the downs of His ministry. Salome knew it. She is believed to be the mother of James and John, the Zebedee boys, who wanted a special place for her sons in this new kingdom. Jesus looked through her doubt, through her narrow and naked ambition, and saw her potential and her zeal.

No wonder they made their way. Hear the text. "And very early on the first day of the week, when the sun had risen, they went to the tomb." They had been saying to one another, "Who will roll away the stone for us from the entrance to the tomb?" I like these women because they are aware of the stone. Yet, they refuse to use the stone as a stumbling block. They are able to face the facts and hold onto their faith at the same time. Most people consider the facts, and it freezes their faith. These individuals are carnal. Others seem to believe that to be a person of faith is to be in denial about the facts. They are naïve. I like these women because they are able to face the facts and hold onto their faith at the same time. They are worried and wondering and walking at the same time. They don't know how they're going to get into the tomb, but they go anyhow. And sometimes you have to go on anyhow, walk on anyhow, work on anyhow, press on anyhow, and pray on anyhow. That's how you break through barriers. You have to go on anyhow!

They go on, but they are clear about the barriers and the odds that confront them. That's why they are asking, "Who will roll away the stone?" And, in a world like ours, that's a good question. Who will roll away the stone? In other words, who will do the heavy lifting? Not the light stuff, but the heavy lifting! In other words, who will tackle the big issues and address themselves and their work to the complex problems? In a war-torn world, who will give peace and diplomacy a real chance? In a nation that imprisons more people than any other nation, who will reform a criminal justice system whose racially disparate outcomes are too often more criminal than just? Who will do the heavy lifting? In a world where cheating public school teachers and administrators get bail, and cheating mortgage brokers and Wall Street bankers get bailouts, who will do the heavy lifting? Will we simply flog them as convenient scapegoats, or will we get serious about doing what's necessary to give all of our children a real chance? Who will do the heavy lifting? When it's time to plan ministry, not for the last century, but for the twenty-first century, who will do the heavy lifting? When the money is short, and the bills are due, who will do the heavy lifting? Now that daddy's died and mama's gone, who will do the heavy lifting?

I don't know where the men are. But these women get up early in the morning because they know they've got work to do. They don't know how or who but somebody's got to roll the stone away! Are you someone who has been stuck? Have you been hanging on a dilemma, and you don't know how or who, but somebody's got to do something about the stone and the stumbling block in your way?

Well, they just start walking even while they're talking. Some folk just talk. Others walk. They are walking and talking. Hoping and praying. Doubting and believing at the same time. Planning and working. They are operating in the already even while living in the not yet. That's what faith is. It is operating in the already even while living in the not yet. And guess what? When they get there, the stone "which was very large, had already been rolled back." If you start, God will finish. But God can't finish what you won't start! When they got there, "the stone had already been rolled back." He's rolling it back. Yes, He is! He's rolling it back!

God rolled it back; not so Jesus could get out, but so they could get in! Don't you know that He who descended into hell in order to hold captivity captive could not be contained in a tomb? They were on the outside, but now they're on the inside. God breaks through barriers. He started from the bottom, so that we all can rise to the top. God breaks down barriers, so others can succeed in life and fulfill their divine purpose.

And, as they entered the tomb, they saw a young man, dressed in a white robe, sitting on the right side. He said to them, "Do not be alarmed; you are looking for Jesus…of Nazareth…who was crucified." "He has been raised. He is not here." Look, there is the place they laid Him. That's the place. But where He was is not where He is. Some of you are stuck in the same place. That's where He was. But where He was is not where He is. God is moving all the time!

The angel says tell His disciples and tell Peter that He has risen from the dead. Why does he single out Peter? Peter is a disciple. Yet, he says, tell his disciples and Peter. You remember, Peter denied Him. And the last time Jesus saw Peter, he was weeping bitterly over what he had done. The messenger says tell Peter that he may have denied Jesus, but Jesus never gave up on him. Tell Peter that there is nothing about his past or your past that God's grace and God's mercy cannot penetrate! I'm God and I can break through every barrier and every chain!

"He is going ahead of you to Galilee; there you will see him." When you finally get enough nerve to go where you're going, you will discover that God has already gotten there and is waiting on you to arrive. You're not waiting on God. God is waiting on you! Break through the barriers of your own anxiety and fear and insecurity and questions and pain and pressure and bruises and hurt feelings and disappointments and doubt and meet Him in Galilee! If you walk toward God, God will run to meet you! If you try to touch God, God will touch you! If you reach out to God, God will embrace you! Yes He will!

A Divine Deterrent
Delores James Cain
2 Corinthians 12: 7-9

Have you ever had something to irritate you to the very core of your soul? I'm talking about a nagging, gnawing, and negative circumstance that caused you to cry out to God. Perhaps it was a diagnosis of multiple sclerosis or diabetes with neuropathy. Maybe it is a child who has an addiction that has seemed to destroy his or her life and devastate the family, and you have tried to help, prayed, cried and ask the prayers of the church but the addiction is still there, and it takes you to your knees constantly. But after crying out many years later, it was still there? How do you reconcile problems and pain so heavy that they cause you to cry out to God for relief and yet he does not take the pain away? How do you rationalize a disease or condition that requires constant hospitalizations that treat the condition but never cures? The book of 2 Corinthians 12: 7-9 has been tailored to talk to us about some possible reasons why we suffer pain and problems and our response when some problems don't go away.

In this text, Paul continues to address an issue – begun in chapter 11 – concerning his inferiority to other apostles, and what we might today call spiritual heavyweights. The spiritual heavyweights boasted in their gifts and used their gifts to increase their personal standing among the people. So Paul, in the first six verses, outlines the wondrous things that he has experienced in the spirit of which he could boast, but has chosen not to do as he tells us why. Paul recalls a vision of being raptured into the third heaven, and while there he heard things that were not lawful to utter. In other words, it was just for him. Paul's statement is something we can learn for free. He teaches that there are things that God reveals to you, that is for your consolation but not for your communication. It is just for you. However, in this sermon text, beginning in the 7th verse, Paul reveals to us a secret of how God uses the devices of Satan to accomplish His Will through us…

He paints for us why he will not boast, *"And lest I should be exalted above measure through the abundance of the revelations, there was given to me a thorn in the flesh, the messenger of Satan to buffet me, lest I should be exalted above measure."* (2 Corinthians 12:7, KJV)

Notice that the first thing we discover about this thorn in the flesh is that; it was given to him. These spiritual heavyweights attacked the reputation and worth of Paul and his comrades because they were suffering. There were problems in Paul's life, and his accusers charged that the reason for the suffering was because of deceitful work. Paul stipulates that he had not done anything to cause the thorn, but he quantifies the thorn as a gift because of the spiritual heights he has experienced because of it. It is as if he says to them that his spiritual walk has created for him a thorn to keep him grounded. I also see him saying to them that spiritual heights require God to move to assure that you don't self exalt and steal His glory.

The second thing we see about the thorn is that it was in the flesh. It was a real issue, not spiritual. Paul wasn't talking about some trivial issue or sin weakness. If the issue were sinful, God would remove it because it is His Will that we walk in holiness and be imitators of Jesus Christ. When our prayers line up with His Will, the faithfulness of His Word can be counted upon to meet our request. So here we learn that the thorn was given; it was in the flesh; and it was quite possibly a physical condition that was not going away. Some of us experience physical conditions that are thorns in our flesh. We have diabetes, high blood pressure, arthritis, gout and other conditions that cause us to cry out for deliverance.

The third thing we see is that it was from the messenger of Satan; Satan devised it as a gift. The fourth thing we see is its intent: to buffet me.

This word *buffet* means to strike with clenched hands as in fists.

Paul says this thorn is the device of Satan who uses it to strike him with both hands. Also in this seventh verse, we see why it was given. Look at the end of the verse, lest he be *exalted*, meaning, to be raised up, as in *haughty*. The synonyms for haughty, is proud, snooty, arrogant and boastful. Mama would say to "think too highly of yourself." It simply means to *overestimate your worth or value*. Paul says that even when the enemy sends a thorn that strikes me with both hands, I understand the reason why God does not remove it. He allows it because it works together for his overall plan for my life.

Therefore, when we see its purpose and understand that God is in full control of everything in our life including Satan, we must conclude that the thorn is a Divine Deterrent.

Based on what this text has been tailored to teach, we get to our first sermonic point, *A Divine Deterrent is to prevent pride*.

This word for thorn means a tent stake. A tent stake was estimated to be 18 inches in length. So we know it was not just a splinter in the skin but more like a sword in his side. It was long and painful. But, know that this 18-inch stake had a purpose, and it was to anchor the tent during fierce windstorms. The very thing that is a thorn in your flesh is also an anchor.

It prevents pride by anchoring you to the Lord. It keeps us on our knees, wholly dependent on Him to see us through.

We do not know what Paul's thorn was. Some say it was his eyes that watered constantly. What we do know is that it was large and troublesome. It prevents pride by keeping us humble before God.

God will remind us that we are just flesh and blood. We can preach great sermons and sing melodious songs, but lest we become arrogant and proud and forget whose we are and why we do what we do, God will allow Satan to send his messenger to beat us up so that we will not get it twisted and start thinking it was us that saved the folks or us that delivered the people. It is God working in us to complete His Will.

God can use anybody to accomplish his work and when he does, we cannot take credit for the outcome. Whatever it takes to keep us humble before him, God will allow. *A Divine Deterrent prevents pride.*

Secondly as we look at the text, we see also that it prompts prayer. Verse 8 says, *for this thing I besought the Lord thrice that it might depart from me.*

Pain and problems prompt us to pray often. Paul prayed three times for God to take the thorn away, and the answer was no. When times are hard, folk will turn to God because they know they cannot help themselves. After September 11th, churches were full because people were fearful of another attack. They felt vulnerable and ran to the only One who could protect them. When Freddie Gray died in the custody of Baltimore police officers and riots broke out all over the city disrupting business and normal everyday functions, resulting in burnt buildings, the nation went in prayer throughout the United States. When nine persons were gunned down in Bible study in Charleston, South Carolina, the nation held prayer vigils all across the country. And when a doctor diagnoses you with a condition you cannot cure or get rid of, you will go to God because He is the only source for your help. Pain and problems prompt us to pray.

But when Paul prayed, God did not remove it. It was not a lack of faith, nor was it because of his sin. God does allow us to contend with some things we would rather do without. Think of Hosea: his wife was a harlot, and yet, he remained a faithful husband to her. Moses had a speech impediment, but God did not remove it – he used him with it. Eli had some wicked sons and God could have changed them, but he used Eli despite his wicked sons. Elizabeth and Zacharias prayed for a son year after year and though the desires of their heart were not fulfilled, Zacharias kept on serving and praying.

Prayer is not about you getting your will done through God, but God getting His Will done through you.

The very thing that is a problem for us pushes us into the presence of God. God says, "You want Me to take away the pain, to solve the problem, to get you out of the situation – but that is not what you need. You need more of Me. The very problem you are seeking to get away from, the very situation you desire to get out of is the very thing that is causing you to stay with Me, spend time with Me, and depend on Me. So, God says to Paul and to us, the answer is no. His Divine Deterrent prompts us to prayer. *A Divine Deterrent prevents pride and prompts prayer.*

Thirdly, *A Divine Deterrent promotes perfection.* It is at verse 9a where God answers Paul. And he said unto me, *My grace is sufficient for thee.* Paul prayed and the Lord answered him. My Grace refers to God's Divine influence. God's Divine influence is in the heart and life of those to whom God shows has shown his loving kindness. This Divine influence impresses the heart to understand that God's grace is sufficient. It promotes perfection in recalling his faithfulness.

Old preachers say, "When you can track his hand, trust his heart. The Divine influence of God works on our heart to remind us of his faithfulness towards us. It reminds us that he has made us some promises that he will keep. We are reminded that he has never left us nor forsaken us. We are reminded that he is a very present help in the time of trouble. It reminds us of the 27th Psalm, *"For in the time of trouble he shall hide me in his pavilion: In the secret of his tabernacle shall he hide me; He shall set me up upon a rock."* (Psalm 27:5, KJV) It is personal. God's Divine influence keeps us in perfect peace in the midst of pain pressures and problems because we are able to recall his faithfulness. A Divine Deterrent promotes perfection in our Reliance on God.

The answer God gave was not the removal of the thorn, but God gave him what he needed. God gave him His favor. Favor may not be fair but it sure is fabulous. When God does not remove the pain or solve the problem, all we can do is to lean and depend on Him. We are left with prayer and praise as we recall what he has already done.

The process of prayer promotes perfection in our ability to wait on God. We discover during those painful, precarious and penetrating moments that God is the only one that can help us. Pastors cannot make the members commit – but God can. Pastors cannot increase the finances and maintain the stability of the tithers, but God can. Pastors cannot make the members get along, but God can. God can use your thorn to press you into prayer until you are perfected in your faith. God can use your thorn until you are perfected in your patience. God can use your thorn to perfect you in peace, love, joy temperance, gentleness, goodness, meekness and faith. Every day that you have to contend with your thorn is another day that you have to rely on God to see you through. The greatest sermon we will ever preach is the one when we cannot do it in our own strength and power. God uses your thorn to promote perfection. He wants to complete you, perfect you in relying solely on Him and realizing that you cannot do this ministry on your own.

We have no choice but to wait on Him because we have tried everything we know and still no success. We are overwhelmed, overpowered and over... trying to do it ourselves. Prayer becomes the vehicle through which we ask, and God answers in due season. But in the meantime – when the times are mean – we are taught to wait and watch. God uses the wait time to call us into agreement with His Will. He uses the wait time to perfect our faith and to perfect our performance. Contending with a Divine Deterrent is a constant reminder that you need the Lord, every second, every minute, every hour of every day. When you are being perfected, which means matured and brought to completion, you have to be tested and approved. God wants to put his stamp of approval on your life. The Mercedes Benz is a great car but it did not become great because of its look – it had to go through a series of tests to be certified and stamped approved to enter into the market. The most important test of the Mercedes is a crash test. The car is approved only after it has been smashed against a wall with a dummy behind the wheel.

And so it is with us. The thorn represents the crashes in our life that served to reveal the flaws in our development. The flaws are already known to God, but unknown to us, so the thorn in the hand of the enemy pushes us to our best performance. The only reason we survived the test is because of the grace of God. You have been through some crashes that should have taken you out – but God used every crash to reveal your imperfect-ness and cause you to agree with Him that you cannot make it by yourself. He will, through grace, perfect you so that you are assured that He is reliable and trustworthy to see you through any and every situation. Even in the midst of pain and problems you discover His grace is always available to you. Therefore you can wait on his power to perfect that, which concerneth you.

Paul prayed until he was changed and with every trial he was perfected until he could write *"Not that I speak in respect of want: for I have learned, in whatsoever state I am, therewith to be content."* (Philippians 4:11, KJV)

God may not give you what you want but he will give you what you need to endure. His grace holds you when turbulent times come, and His grace secures your faith, solidifies your confidence and seals your hope until your change comes because His grace is sufficient. It is good to be in the grip of Grace.

The word *sufficient* in the Greek means *suffice*, to satisfy or to be content.

God says to Paul and to us *"My favor will suffice. My favor will satisfy. My favor will content thee."* I'm glad I have His favor.

The Deterrent God allows Satan to give to you has been designed to mature and complete you. God uses the thorn in your flesh to create discomfort with this world and a longing for our eternal hope. He is perfecting you. The Divine Deterrent prevents pride, prompts prayer, and promotes perfection.

A Divine Deterrent also provides power. Returning to ninth verse where Paul not only says, "My grace is sufficient." He also says. "For my strength is made perfect in weakness. Most gladly therefore will I rather glory in my infirmities, that the power of Christ may rest upon me. Notice that Paul says that my strength is made perfect. God provides power to endure the pain of your problem.

God's strength…is made perfect in weakness.

His strength is fully finished and complete in our weakness. God does his best work when you acknowledge your weakness. The best sermons are preached when you have no strength, the best teaching took place when you pray saying, "Lord – stand up in this tired, worn out flesh of mine for I am weak." The Divine Deterrent is there to remind you that you are frail and full of failure but with the power of God. You are full and you have no lack of faith to trust Him for your next move. When you take your hands off, God will complete the task. When you stop trying to figure it out you will discover that His Grace has worked it out.

God uses Divine deterrents to demonstrate the distinctive difference between a righteous God and a sinful man. The text says, "Most gladly therefore." Something happens to Paul after he has prayed thrice, and still God does not remove his thorn. He comes into agreement with God and acknowledges his helpless estate… and now he is glad.

A Divine Deterrent provides power to alter your attitude.

Paul understands that the thorn in his flesh is a Divine Deterrent that prevents pride, prompts prayer, promotes perfection and presents power so, I most gladly therefore glory (which means to boast) not in my revelations or visions or the work that I have done for Christ, but I boast in my weakness.

The world's philosophy is, "What can't be cured must be endured." But Paul testifies, "What can't be cured can be contented through the power of God's grace." That is why he says in Philippians, "I've learned in whatsoever state I am therewith to be content."

Paul learned how to rejoice in trials and troubles instead of complaining. Why is that? *So, that the power of Christ may rest on me.* Paul says I got it. It is not my brilliance that God wants nor is it my degrees or even my writing skills, but it is my dependence upon his Grace.

To all who shall read this, depend on the power of God's Grace.

God is trying to develop boasting in Him, and He will sometimes use a Divine Deterrent to prevent your pride, prompt your prayer, promote your perfection and present His power. Why not take this time to thank Him for the Divine Deterrent in your life that was accompanied by his grace.

Your Divine Deterrent may be a medical diagnosis or a mental condition.

It may be a physical disability or a financial situation; it may be family and it may be friends, but God can use whatever he chooses to demonstrate to you that His grace is sufficient. I'm grateful for His grace.

When we are weak, God gives us His strength and power. Boast in His strength and be glad that you have His Grace to endure. Boast in Him. Credit your credentials to His grace and His glory, as we look at the final portion of verse nine, so "that the power of Christ" may rest upon you.

This word for rest means to tent upon as to abide.

Remember that the thorn is a picture of a tent stake about 18 inches long. This word for rest is the picture of a tent with the idea of setting up camp or dwelling. Paul rejoices because the power of Christ is abiding with him, like a tent covers those who abide in it.

Paul says with every problem Christ sets His camp upon me, not just in me or around me but upon me, for He covers me. Has Jesus ever covered you? And this thorn, this Divine Deterrent is an anchor to Christ. Everywhere you go He goes with you. Everything you endure, He is with you, with the Deterrent comes His covering? His Grace satisfies.

Paul also rejoices because he is anchored to the power of Christ.

He realizes that the power to endure the thorn is in Jesus. He is grace. So if you succeed it is because of Christ and His strength and not the eloquence of your messages. And if you fall, it is Christ who will restore you... His grace is sufficient. The same power that kept Him on the cross to endure suffering and shame for the sins of the world can also keep you. The same power that kept Him in a grave for three days will keep you through countless lonely and dark days. The same power that raised Him from the dead will raise you up when your enemies come against you. The same power that is given to Him over heaven and earth is given to you to tear down strongholds, to preach and teach Jesus, to make disciples, and to baptize them in the name of the Father and the Son and the Holy Ghost; this grace is yours. So thank Him for the thorns He has sent as a Divine Deterrent to prevent pride, prompt prayer, promote perfection and provide power, and let me add just one more "P." When you understand the power of His grace in the midst of pain, pressures and problems and the purpose of a Divine Deterrent to prevent pride, prompt prayer, promote perfection and provide power, it ought to provoke praise. God has used your pain as a means of showing you the power of His grace.

Praise Him that with every thorn you can stake a claim to the power of Jesus Christ that is deep and strong. Praise Him that with every thorn, we are reminded of the debt we owe.

- His tent, your stake.
- His cross, your salvation,
- His blood your sanctification,
- His resurrection, your unlimited access to his power
- His ascension, your seat in Heavenly places

Thank God for using a Divine Deterrent to prevent pride, prompt prayer, promote perfection and provide power... so that you might have more than enough reason to praise Him. Adversity is just one more chance for you to experience the mighty power of God in your life. The thorn causes Jesus to stay close. I can say like the songwriter, *though the storms keep on raging in my life – my soul has been anchored in the Lord.*

A Dialogue With Death
Johnny Ray Youngblood
Luke 24:6-7

This is the news dropped by some celestial messengers to some sorrowing sisters who had made their way to the Savior's sepulcher on a given Sunday morning.

The angels said to the sisters, *"He is not here, but is risen."*

And the only explanation offered by these celestial creatures is in the form of the memory-jolting pronouncement found in verses 6b and 7, where they said, *"Remember how He spake unto you when He was yet in Galilee, saying, The Son of man must be delivered into the hands of sinful men and be crucified, and the third day rise again."*

In other words, my brothers and sisters, I hear the angels saying to the ladies, "Didn't He tell y'all He wasn't going to be here?"

You see, my brothers and sisters, when the S-U-N rose that morning, the S-O-N had already risen.

These sisters and certain others were already suffering from the horrible hangover of Jesus' crucifixion. They had, under extreme anguish, recognized the historic Sabbath. And now, motivated by that love that defies even the power of death, they beat a path to the burial site of Jesus. There, as the victims of honest unbelief and pitifully short memories, they discovered the missing corpus delicti. They found the stone rolled away, but reasoned that some of the bereaved who arrived earlier had moved the stone. But then, after the discovery that the body was not there, John's record and Mark's memoirs implied that so sinister were the protectors of the status quo - the Roman government - that one of the women concluded that the corpse had been confiscated. "They have stolen my Lord's body."

Then, they were informed by an angelic presence, *"He is not here, but is risen."*

Can't y'all hear it? The Angel is implying, "You're not at the wrong tomb, sisters. He was here; He just ain't here now. No one has taken Him. Though you're early, you're late! You woke up early, but He rose even earlier. Sisters, not only has the S-U-N risen as it is accustomed to do, but just like He said He would, the S-O-N has also risen."

WHAT HAPPENED AT THE TOMB?

Now, my brothers and sisters, I am a spiritual snoop. Whenever I read the Scriptures, I'm always looking for some spiritual scoop. I wanted to know what happened. I needed more information than that which came from some creatures from another realm telling these sisters, "He is not here, He is risen." Somebody, I felt, needed to give more information on my Savior than just the statement, "He is not here, but is risen." I wanted to know what happened. I know that He'd already said He wasn't going to be a permanent resident of the silent city. I know He said that! And I know He had never been caught coming up short on His word. But I still feel as a member of the family that, especially by faith, there's got to be more of an explanation to the missing corpus delicti than just some creature from another realm coming along making the announcement, "He is not here, but is risen." And so, I am determined in the power of the Spirit that somebody must talk to me about my Savior's missing body.

Let's examine for a few minutes who was on the scene.

One writer reports that some soldiers were there, but they were so awe-stricken and amazed that they couldn't believe it; and their employers couldn't believe it either. Also, they had been ordered and paid to lie about the disappearance of the body. So we can't talk to the soldiers.

How about the angels themselves? No. Forget the Angels. Don't try to talk to the angels because, you see, they are messengers of the Most High, and most of their appearances in the Scriptures are characterized as monologues. They do not entertain the queries of the creature; they merely deliver the message of the Creator.

How about Simon Peter? Naw. Remember, he followed him from afar off.

Andrew? No! He was Simon Peter's youngest brother, always in Simon's shadow. So, most probably, he followed a little farther off.

What about Nicodemus? Nicodemus was probably somewhere moving under the shadows of the night.

And the women visitors? Remember they got there after the fact.

Is there really anybody with whom we can talk about our Lord's missing body?

Let me explain to you one of the reasons why I'm determined to talk to somebody. There is talk of an alleged/speculated resurrection. And if such was the case, God was in on it. If God was in on it, He never leaves

Himself without a witness. So, the logic of faith concludes that there's got to be a witness somewhere who can testify to what went down between sunset Friday and sunrise Sunday morning.

Q AND A WITH MR. DEATH

"God! Oh, God! God, with whom can we talk about our Lord's missing body? With whom can we talk about this corpus delicti that disappeared? With whom can we talk, God? Would you direct us to 'the witness' for a little while?"

And God says, "Why not talk to the star witness?" "The star witness?" we reply. And God says, "Yes, the star witness who is also the chief victim!"

Lord, do you mean Death? Oh, yeah! Death, the now stingless victimizer of the living. Death had to be there!

Wow! God Almighty is granting us an interview with the landlord of the household of the lifeless. Think about it: divinity allows dust to dialogue with Death. Let us take advantage of this opportunity.

"Mr. Death? Oh, Mr. Death, the Sovereign has granted us mortals permission to engage in an interview with you for faith's sake. We want to know about the conflict on Calvary.

"Now, Mr. Death, we know you're busy. The hearse wheels keep on rolling. We know you're busy. The church bells keep on tolling. We know you're busy. The obituary rolls are steadily swelling, and many cemeteries are plagued by over population. Mr. Death, we know you're busy. Your movements are reported by the newspapers, relayed by the radio and beamed out on worldwide TV. Mr. Death, we know you're busy. But for faith's sake, the Lawyer of the land has given us permission to talk with you for a few minutes about what went down first-hand in the incident on Calvary."

Q: Oh, Mr. Death, pardon us for staring at you and for being a bit personal. But, Mr. Death, while looking at you, we noticed that you're not made up like other creatures. You lack certain anthropomorphic features. Mr. Death, there's some regions of your being that cannot be spoken of in anatomical terms. Mr. Death, why are you made up the way you're made up? You are a rather grotesque-looking creature. Why are you made up the way you are?

A: I'm made up the way I am in order that discrimination might not be one of my abilities. You see, I'm blind. I have no place for eyes or eye sockets in order that color consciousness might not control me. I'm blind in order that social status will be of no effect. You can be as white as the drifting snow. You can be as red as crimson or as yellow as the noonday sun. If you're from Mars, you can be as green as grass. If you're black, you can be as black as a thousand midnights down in a cypress swamp. But when it's your time to go, your color does not sway me. I'm blind in order that social status might not control me. I've pulled princes from thrones, and I've pulled paupers from gutters. I've got access to every house in the universe. I've got access to the White House, the courthouse, and the church house. I've even got access to your house. I'm blind in order that discrimination might not be one of my abilities.

But not only that, since you're asking, look close and you will see that there is no place for ears of any kind of hearing apparatus. I'm deaf in order that last-minute negotiations might not sway me. See, I can't hear, "Wait." I can't hear, "No... I'd like to see my children grow up." I can't hear, "Give me one more chance." I can't hear, "Let me get my house in order." I am not Opportunity. I never knock twice – maybe once. To be honest, I don't have to knock at all. No notices necessary. I just show up.

And in case you don't recognize it, look closer since you want to know something about me, and the Almighty has given me permission to talk to y'all. If you had a stethoscope, that medical instrument, and you used it in that region that's normally known as the upper torso, you will discover that I'm also without a heart. I'm heartless. I don't have any regard for blood bonds. I'll snatch parents from children and children from parents. I've got no qualms about depriving nations of leaders. I'm heartless. I don't care who you are, how old you are, what you mean to somebody, or what you don't mean to anybody. When it's your time to go, it's your time to go."

Q: Thank you, Mr. Death, for those sobering realities. Would you talk with us a little bit about your background?

A. Well, Adam's rebellious act made room for me in creation. Haven't you read what it says in your Scriptures? Don't y'all remember? By sin came death into the world? And my presence and power has since been recognized. Why, since my debut, it has been once appointed unto all men to die. I've written that into the equation of human history. You see, what y'all need to accept is that I walk hand-in-hand with life. You don't die because you're old. You don't die because you're knifed by a maniac or you're struck by a drunken driver. You die because you are alive. If you don't want to die, then you don't want to live. You can't have a life without dying. That senior citizen at 80 is dying no faster than the junior citizen at 18. The senior might be 80, and the junior might be 18; but one merely starts earlier and the other one leaves a little later. The clock ticks away the same measured seconds for one as it does the other. And while I know you have the hope of being caught up to meet Him, you don't know whether or not that's going to be your arrangement. Most of you have a date with death and reservations in a cemetery somewhere.

Q: **What are some of your affiliations?**

A: **Well, since Calvary, I've worked for God and the Devil, but a whole lot of y'all work for me.** Lee Harvey Oswald worked for me, and Sirhan Sirhan worked for me. James Earl Ray worked for me. John Wilkes Booth worked for me. Adolph Hitler worked for me. Judas Iscariot worked for me. Some of the slavemasters worked for me. You need to know that each man and woman holds within their hands the power of death over another man. All of y'all somehow or another can kill each other. If you don't do it with a knife or a gun, there is a little pound of flesh that is a deadly weapon, locked up in the maximum security of 32 teeth. And even your Bible informs you that the power of life and death is in the tongue. Yeah, some of y'all work for me, and I've worked for God and the Devil since Calvary."

Q: **Mr. Death, how do you see yourself?"**

A: **Well, I've got a good record – a pretty influential reputation.** It's not perfect, especially since Calvary, but I've got a good record. Upon my release from the solitary confinement of that tree in the center of the Garden of Eden, I got the run of the land. My debut was made when Cain, hostile toward his brother, sponsored me in that open field. And after that I got Abraham, Isaac, Ishmael, and Jacob; I got Moses and Aaron; I got Saul, David, and Solomon; I got Isaiah, Jeremiah, and Ezekiel. Hezekiah got a 15-year extension, but I got him in the end. And y'all rave about Methuselah who lived 969 years, but I still got him. In fact, you know what y'all need to know? Y'all need to know that I have an office in the halls of justice in heaven, and God – from time to time – calls a caucus on you mortals. And when He calls a caucus on y'all, I'm invited to the meeting with voting rights. I was there when we caucused on Belshazzar, and I got him. We caucused on Jezebel, and I got her. We caucused on Bull Connor, and I got him. We caucused on Saul of Tarsus, but mercy beat me out. We caucused on George Wallace, but it was a split decision; mercy almost beat me out. I got only his legs for a season, but in the end I got all of him. But y'all, I still got a good record. I got Ezekiel, I got Micah, I got Hosea, I got Isaiah, and I got Joel. I also got Matthew, Mark, Luke, and John. I finally got Paul, Timothy, John, and Mark. I got John F. Kennedy, Robert Kennedy, Abe Lincoln, along with Martin and Alberta King. I got a whole bunch of folks.

Q: But Mr. Death, haven't you missed a few?

A: Yeah, but you can't prove it. You're talking about Moses and Elijah, with their strange disappearances.

Q: Yeah, But there are some others, Mr. Death.

A: Who?

Q: Lazarus, Jairus' daughter, the son of the widow from Nain, and that Tishbite boy. Didn't you miss them?

A: I missed them one time. But, Youngblood, I got them on the second go-round. What y'all need to know is my record was all right until I got to Calvary.

Q: Mr. Death, we want to go there in a few minutes. But just one more question in terms of our preliminaries. Mr. Death, what is man's opinion of you?

A: I'm well respected; I'm even influential. Don't y'all know that it isn't until I threaten that some men get right with God? It isn't until I threaten that folk recognize they've been wasting time and been mistreating one another. It isn't until I threaten that folks recognize the folly of riches and the limitations of family and friendship. When I threaten, a whole lot of y'all have gotten right with God. I'm well respected. And I'm influential.

Q: Well, last but not least, Mr. Death, we want to know what happened on Calvary. Mr. Death, you're kind of dropping what looks like your head. What happened on Calvary?

A: Well, since God has ordered this dialogue, I have to tell you the truth, the whole truth, nothing but the truth, so help me. I can really sum it up in six words. **I had no business being there.**

Q: Say what, Mr. Death?

A: I had no business being there."

Q: What do you mean, Mr. Death?

A: Look, Justice moved that I should be responsible for dealing with those two men on those two outside crosses. Now, based on that, I should have been there, but I shouldn't have messed with that man on that middle cross. I hate I ever messed with Him. In fact, since I've got to tell y'all about it, I was so mixed up that Friday I didn't know who I worked for – God or the Devil. But what you've got to understand is that those perverted politicians and those religious racketeers were always so willing to sponsor me that I took advantage of every opportunity to make my presence felt. But y'all, I shouldn't have messed with that man on that middle cross.

Q: What happened, Mr. Death?

A: He gave me a fit.

Q: What? We want some detail, Mr. Death.

A: Well, since some of y'all claim you know your Bible, don't you remember that the wages of sin is death? And he was without sin. So, since He was without sin I had no business messing with Him because the wages of sin was death and He was sinless. Not only that, don't y'all remember the promise from Moses' 90th psalm – that the days of our years are three score years and ten (70), and if by reason of strength they be fourscore (80); yet is there strength, labor and sorrow. He was only 33. So based on the promise, I had no business messing with Him. Not only that, I couldn't even use His body as a vehicle on which to have disease to ride in order that His life might be snuffed out because He had more medicine in the hem of His garment than all the drugstores in town. What happened was this: I went up to Calvary that Friday, and I grabbed all three of them. Y'all, that man in the middle gave me a fit to the point that I had to let everybody else go just to deal with Him.

Let me tell you what He did to me, since I've got to testify. Let me tell y'all what He did to me. First of all, He wouldn't let me sneak up on Him. They tried to give Him something to numb His body – some anesthesia in order that I could sneak up and take Him away, but He wouldn't take it. In fact, when I went up, I rushed Him and blitzed Him. When I grabbed Him, He knocked me back and said, "No man takes my life; I lay it down." He wouldn't drink the potion that was given Him to numb His body. He wanted to present His body as a living sacrifice, holy and acceptable unto God which was His reasonable service. He wouldn't let me sneak up on Him.

And then I was there trying to kill Him, and He was up there taking care of business. I'm there trying to take His life and He's up there giving.

Q: What do you mean, Mr. Death?

A: Well, don't y'all remember that while He was hanging on the cross, He stopped dying and gave a thief last-minute reservations on the evening train to Paradise? And then that wasn't enough. He stopped and gave the whole world forgiveness. He said, "Father, forgive them for they know not what they do." And then, as though that wasn't enough, He looked down and gave his mama to John and John to his mama. I was there trying to take and He was up there giving.

And when I grabbed Him, I really grabbed Him. I grabbed Him, y'all, I'm telling you. When I grabbed Him, I had already let the two thieves on the outside crosses go. But when I grabbed Him I had to send for backup. And when I sent for backup, I had to let everybody else that I ever had go. That's why John wrote that the dead got up and went walking through the streets of Jerusalem. I had to release Abraham. Abraham reached over and shook Isaac and Isaac, Ishmael; Ishmael, Jacob; Jacob, Esau; Esau, Moses; Moses, Aaron; Aaron, Saul; Saul, David; David, Solomon.... They all got up and started walking through the streets of Jerusalem. That's what it took for me to hold Him. I got Him. I had to let everybody else go, but I got Him. But, I could only hold Him from sunset Friday to sunrise Sunday morning.

Q: Then what happened?

A: Since I got to tell y'all the whole truth, nothing but the truth, let me tell you something that was so amazing. When I grabbed Him and it was time for Him to get up, the angels got in a hurry and wanted to come quickly. The speediest angel – somebody said his name was Raphael, I don't know – came and he said to God, "Let me go down and get your Son." And God the Father said, "Oh, no! That's My son. I'm handling this!" And that's another reason why Paul wrote to the church at Rome – that God has raised Him from the dead. God raised Him! The angels may have rolled the stone away, but God raised Him. In my native Louisiana, they said that when they buried Him, they put a rock in a rock; and then they rolled a rock on top of a rock. Then, on Sunday morning when God the Father got ready to raise Him, He rolled a rock away from a rock; and there was a rock in a rock. And then a rock woke up in a rock and a rock looked up at a rock, and then a rock stepped out on a rock.

Q: We all know that story.

A: Yes, but you just don't know the intimate details that I'm giving you in this moment. When He stepped out of the grave, ah, your Savior got sassy. He stepped out of the grave, shook my dust off, looked back, said, "Death, where's your sting? Grave, where's your victory?" And then He raised His hands and pronounced the benediction for all time when He declared, "All power..." Do y'all know what "all" means? It means, "All power is in My hands."

That's why when the women arrived that morning, they were told, "He ain't here. He's risen. He was here, but He's not here now." The reason the tomb is empty is I just couldn't hold onto Him any longer. These are the unyielding facts – that you serve a risen Savior.

I know that many of you have crosses around your neck. You also have crosses in your house and everywhere. But the cross was the instrument of the Enemy. The real instrument of victory for the believer is not the cross but the empty tomb. To the cross they nailed His hands, riveted His feet, and placed a crown of thorns on His head. The Cross!

There were three men crucified in that moment, but only one got up!

That's why the resurrection makes all the difference.

RISEN MEANS "ALIVE AND WELL"

Well, this concludes our interview with Death. We thank God for condoning this dialogue. I urge all of us to recognize that we serve a risen Savior. He did die, but He didn't stay dead. They did crucify Him, but He got up from the grave and He's risen. He's risen, as He said.

You know what risen means? Risen means "alive and well." Risen – victorious conqueror. Risen – offering new hope to all men. Risen – disarming the last enemy. Risen – King of kings. Risen – Lord of lords. Risen – no corpus delicti. Risen – an empty tomb. Risen – neatly folded grave clothes, which showed that He wasn't in a hurry when He got up. Risen – absentee tenant. Risen – a displaced stone.

As the hymn says,

I serve a risen Savior. He's in the world today;
I know that He is living, whatever men may say;
I see His hand of mercy, I hear His voice of cheer,
And just the time I need Him He's always near.

He lives, He lives, Christ Jesus lives today!
He walks with me and talks with me along life's narrow way.
He lives, He lives, salvation to impart!
*You ask me how I know He lives? He lives within my h*eart

But not only that: He walks with me, watches over me all night. I serve a risen Savior. Thank you, Lord, for Bethlehem. Thank you, Lord, for Calvary. But above all, thank you for the empty tomb. He ain't there – He's risen. Risen! Risen! Risen! Risen! He's risen.

I Gotta Let It Go!
Tyrone P. Jones IV
Judges 11: 1-11, 30-38

It is important that we learn to let some things go. Eleanor Roosevelt said "The future does not belong to those who allow there past to define them, but the future belongs to those who would dare to dream despite your difficulties." One of the most devastating things we could ever do is to allow our past experiences to detain us, define us, and/or deter us.

This is one the main reasons why, in Joshua 1:1, the text says, "After the death of Moses, the Lord spoke to Joshua and said Moses my servant is Dead!" (Did you get that!). The book of Jude says that God buried Moses, God gave the eulogy and the final committal just 30 days ago, but God found it necessary to tell Joshua "Moses my servant is dead!" The emphasis hear is on the fact that a reluctant Joshua needed a word to remind him to NOW let go of your past, so that it will not block or hinder your future.

This is a critical time in all of our lives and it's going to be important that you release your past in order to embrace your future!! Learn To Let It Go!!

1. Your Past Cannot Determine Your Future, Or Deter you From Your Destiny

Your past must not, should not, cannot define you, it was just a temporary stop on your way to your destiny.

This obscure text tells us about a man that not many people know about or even really preach about. The text tells us about a man named Jephthah (Jeff-Tha). Now what is interesting is that text says that Jephthah was born to a distinguished father named Gilead, but his mother was a prostitute. His father was a married to another woman, but (Jeff-Tha's) mother was a harlot. That means in a moment of temporary weakness his father had an affair that produced the son who was deemed an outsider. One who was not accepted…

In fact, the Bible said that Jephthah's brothers drove him away. His brothers kicked him to the curb. This brother could get no love from his brothers because Jephthah represented the pain of his family's past indiscretions. (Jeff-Tha represented 3 things)

A. Jephthah was a disturbing reminder. Every time he walked through his father's house, he was reminder of his father's failures. Every time he sat down to eat dinner they were reminded of their father's messy morals. He was the embodiment of some past mistakes that have been made permanent and public!!! Sometimes we can be the disturbing reminder of some muddy and messy issues, even though you really didn't do anything wrong, you can be seen as a sobering reminder!

B. Jephthah was also of a different race. Because prostitution was outside the Mosaic Law scholar suggest that Gilead had an encounter with a woman of a different ethnicity. This probably made Jephthah look different from his brothers. The hue of his skin was probably different due to his ethnic background. The reality is we all live in a place where race still matters. However, people of the Kingdom of God are not suppose to be concerned about what is on the outside, we are supposed to be brothers and sisters based on what is on the inside. In church, race is not supposed to matter.

C. They were afraid that Jephthah would be a dreadful representation. The text tells us that Jephthah was the eldest brother, and so if the mantle of leadership fell on him as the oldest brother would (Jeff-Tha) be able to represent them well. They had no faith in his leadership abilities, based on the parameters of his past, the make up of his parentage, the potential of his position.

Sometimes, people will mishandle you, simply because you are different and to others you can be just as dreadful and disturbing, BUT my past still cannot determine my destination!!!

D. They were also scared that Jephthah would be a disastrous replica. The family was think if we allow you to lead us, what's to stop you from making the same mistakes that daddy made. And sometime people will judge us based upon the missteps and mistakes of somebody else.

Remember that none of this was Jephthah's fault! Somebody needs to know that negative nature of your past was not your fault. God wants you to know that you had nothing to do with this, but you are going to see that God has everything to do with you!!

The question that we should remember is not who's fault is it, but the question is how is God going to get the glory out of it? How will these gory details, become glorious deeds?

Remember in John 9, the question was asked to Jesus who sinned was it the blind man's parents, who sinned in this case?? Jesus responded,

"Nobody sinned, this happened, he was born this way **so that God can get the Glory!!"**

The question is not whose fault it is, but how will God get glory from it!

Watch this! Verse 1 says that Jephthah was a mighty warrior! Now this is important because this is not a word about who Jephthah is externally, but really this is an internal declaration of who God created him to be! Please don't miss this!! When we study the text we find that this proclamation was listed but Jephthah had never gone to battle before!!!!

But it is only after he has his encounter with his brothers that Jephthah goes to battle!! So what does this mean? That he was already a "Mighty Warrior!" It means that he got credit for the internal battles of his past, and this gave him the internal fortitude to press despite what he faced. The greatest battles that some of us will ever fight are not the battles that are raging on the outside of us, but it those internal battles that you have had to fight on the inside of you. This means your past was a set up from the inside out to propel you past your past, and into your future position!!

That means that Jephthah had the courage to move on despite the issues of his past!! People will let you down, but you move on up! People will kick you to the curb, but you got to move on up! You are a mighty warrior!!

A warrior is one who can go through difficulty and challenges and keep it moving!!

A warrior is somebody who doesn't allow there past to eclipse their future!! Come what may! Winds may blow! Seasons may change! People can act funny, but I am more than a conqueror in Christ Jesus!!

2. It is important to understand that your Past cannot deter you from your destiny, and secondly, People cannot deter you from your Destiny!

No matter how bad people may treat you, please understand that people cannot stop what God has for you! (Don't miss your shout cue!)

Does it seems like every time you turn around you keep running into difficult people! OK, I thought I had some help, OK maybe they are sitting on your row and you don't want to call them out... Sometimes people can be some of the most cantankerous, argumentative, obstinate, vile, mean, conniving, evil and down right nastiest folk in the world, and then they will and tell you bless the Lord!!!

Just remember they cannot stop what God has begun! He who has begun a good work in you, will continue to perform it until the day of Jesus Christ!! (Phil. 1:6)

In our text, it is interesting that his brothers kick him out, and they send him to a land called Tob!! Somebody say Tob, and his brothers thought that Tob was going to break him. But God ordained it to be that Tob would not break him, but that Tob would turn around and bless him!! Tob was like the Alcatraz of that day! It was a place of imprisonment. In Tob, there was nothing but murders, mercenaries, thieves and outlaws. Some translations called this a colony or band of wild men.

Watch This! His brothers thought not only are we going to kick you out, but also we are going to send you to a place that is going to totally just mess you up for life. But what was meant to break him, blessed him!! Tob blessed Jeff-Tha 3 ways!

A. Tob blessed Jephthah in a Personal Way. Jephthah was supposed to be the next Judge of Israel, but he could never embrace what God had for him because he was so enamored by his need to be accepted by his brothers!! So instead of pursuing God's destiny for his life, he allowed his destiny and identity to be wrapped in what his brother thought. So the best thing that God can do personally, is to some time rearrange our places, rearrange our positions and rearrange some people in our lives, until we get the hint to keep our focus on God!! God knows that unless we are removed from those that we have placed our sole trust in, as it relates to our destiny, we will never get to our place of purpose that God has for our us!! Tell somebody that God is a People Mover!! (Somebody said while man plays checkers, God always plays chess!! People will try to move you quick, to stack the deck against you, but God's moves are strategic where with Him you can win the whole board, with just few calculated moves.)

God said, I cannot allow your future to rest on whether or not people like you or not. I cannot allow your future to be in the hands of the feeble and fickleness of people. I cannot allow your future to rest on whether or not somebody invites you be apart of their click. I cannot allow your future to rest on whether or not you get invited to somebodies house or not. But I will personally take what you were handed, and make it better for you!!

B. Tob also blessed Jephthah to meet the right People. Now he was surrounded by murders, mercenaries, thieves, and other so called menace to society. (v.3) But the text tells us that it was in Tob that Jephthah got married and had a family in Tob. It amazing how God will bless us in the places where we least expect it!! That means no matter where we are it is important to associate with people based on purpose, and not based on type! Your type maybe tall, dark, and handsome, but your person with purpose maybe short, fat, and strange!! Learn to connect with people who aligned with your purpose, and not your type! In other words, learn to love those, who love you! Stop seeking the love of somebody that don't even want to be bothered with you! Love the one with!

C. Tob blessed Jephthah Providentially. Get this, his brothers thought that Tob was going to break him. His brother kicked him out to this place. But God, providentially, turned around what was bad and made it work for his good! All thing work together for the good to those who love God and are called according to His purpose!!! God turns it around... Watch This! The word Tob in the Hebrew means GOOD! So when the Bible says that he settled in the land of Tob, this literally means that he settled in the land of GOOD!

This means that on the surface it may look like a messed up situation, but in reality it's really all GOOD, in my neighborhood!! On the surface, this may have looked like a jack-up situation that was undesirable, but beneath the surface God says, I know exactly where I am taking you!! I know exactly what I am doing in your life.

Where you are going may not be attractive, but it is a place that will mess around and grow you!! This is the perfect place to birth what I have in you. God providentially put us in this place, because it is a good place for purpose!!

So the next time somebody tells you that it can't be done it, it can't happen, it can't work, it won't work, good over to them and tell them thank you!! Because sometimes God does His greatest work in the most unusual ways.

I am going to give you one more point! So your past cannot deter you from your destiny. People cannot deter you from your destiny...

3. Finally, Be careful not to let prior failures implode your destiny!!

The text reveals that Jephthah is doing well in Tob. He has gotten married, he has a family and new friends, but then his brothers come rolling back into his life, after they got rid of him. Its like that friend who dismissed only to come back after you are successful and they turn around and tell you, "Hey, I knew you had it in you all the time!"

He doing well, but when they come back all they do is re-introduce the pain that they represented!! They did come back to say how impressed they were with him, and with all that he had accomplished. These brothers come to Jephthah because they needed him. Be careful when people show up in your life, not because they care for you, but because of what they can get out of you. The come back and ask him to lead them! Would you lead us and become our commander.

This is a test to see if God can trust you, especially when people of your past start coming back into your life. How you handle people from your past says a lot about how much you really trust God leading and the people that you now have in your life. Jephthah is faced with a conundrum. Do I stay here, or do I go back with them!

He was still seeking others approval, and they baited him with leading the clan against the Ammonites. He wants to go back and be a baller so bad that he winds up making this rash vow with God! He said, if you make me victorious, the first thing that comes out of my house, I will sacrifice to you (v. 30-31).

He wants the approval of the wrong people so bad that he was willing to sacrifice the right people!!!

God allows him to be victorious over the Ammonites, and when he returns, who is first person to come out of the house? It his daughter – his only child – the right person comes dancing and celebrating. She was so proud of his accomplishments. When he sees her, he tears his clothes. Why? Because he recognizes that there was lingering stuff in his past that made him make a rash vow unto God!

In longing to please the wrong people, now he has to sacrifice the right people. Let me tell you this, no one else has to die, because Jesus was willing to die!!! Look the good news in all of this is if you learn to let go! Your marriage doesn't have to be sacrificed. Your family doesn't have to be sacrificed. Your children don't have to be sacrificed. Your dreams don't have to be sacrificed. Your future doesn't have to be sacrificed. Because we have a Savior that has already done all the sacrificing we need.

So, stop trying to hold on to those who have rejected you! Stop trying to seek the approval of those who really don't matter! Stop allowing negative thoughts to rule your daily decisions!

Who is in Jephthah's shoes? I have come to tell you to let go of the stuff from your past and be free to live the future that God intended for you to have. Let it GO!!!

Good News In A Culture Of Violence: How To Stop A Funeral Procession
Earl Payton
Luke 7:11-17

When one considers the world we live in today – not just the United States, it is obvious that we live in a culture of violence that frequently leads to death, and it occurs in cities, states and regions far and wide. A verdict was pronounced in Detroit, Michigan regarding the case of a young African American American woman whose car experienced a mechanical breakdown. She stopped to knock on the door of a white man's home to ask for help, and he shot and killed her. **We live in a culture of violence.**

In South Africa, a trial involving a white Olympic athlete who shot and killed his girlfriend, whom he thought was a burglar. **We live in a culture of violence.**

I love the city of Chicago; I have some great friends there. But in that city, there were 63 shootings reported in one month. Yes, we live in a culture of violence that leads to the death of safe communities.

In the Middle East, there is an increase of new coalitions of violence, storming though Northern Iraq and Syria that has Christians on the run with the threat to "convert or die." One report indicates that these groups have gone so far as to behead children. We live in a culture of violence that leads to the death of innocence.

I served in the United States Army for 22 years as a Chaplain and was stationed in Germany at one point. I remember driving on an autobahn, and it was there that I realized that Germans thought and really believed that they had and have a right to drive fast. Juxtapose that to American culture, where we I feel that we have a right to gun ownership. Most Americans believe it is our constitutional right to own a gun to protect our families and ourselves. We live in culture of violence.

But even in midst of this culture of violence, there is Good News: Luke is the only Gospel that tells the story of the widow Nain that fits into the theme of his concern for the outcast and marginalized. No group was more marginalized in the First century than women, and among them, female widows were the most desperate. According to Jewish custom in the First century, the widow would be at the head of the funeral procession. The Rabbi decreed that women, who brought death into the world, ought to lead the way in the funeral procession. In addition to the grief of having lost her only son, guilty humiliation accompanies the widow as she walks ahead of the crowd. (Card, 98-99)

Here in the text, a procession of Death and Sorrow meets a procession of Life and Hope. Do you see it? There is a funeral convoy of Death and Sorrow: a mother lost her only son and his body is being lead out of the city. Then what I believe to have happened was a collision with another procession! The second procession was lead by Jesus and his disciples. There is a climactic collision between Life and Death in the city of Nain, between light and darkness, between hopelessness and the ultimate hope.

On one hand, here is a young man who has been defeated by death. On the other hand, there is only One who can defeat death! When these two groups ran into each other, they formed a new group! At first there was gloom, doom, grief and groaning. But because of the collision at Nain, outside of the city walls Jesus formed a new group of Victory, Praise and Worship!!

This mother is in the midst of burying her only son. This same mother has already buried her husband, and in the culture and times of the text, this was a devastating undertaking. For as it is mentioned, she is a widow, and death's second invasion of her family took her son and made her future look bleak at best. It was troubling enough to have lost her husband, but now even more suffering comes as she grieves the loss of her only son.

As the woman follows the casket of her son, it appears as though misery and poverty will be everlasting trademarks of her future, as she will unable to care for herself. She is about to enter the place where the least, the lonely and the left out reside. It is not her first choice to remain here; as the text states, she is attending the funeral of her only son. She faced a horrible situation and I want to suggest that right now, we are dealing with social pathologies in a culture of violence and death. We are simultaneously coping with and trying to understand issues embedded in our culture – the greatest nation on the globe. The United States of America, the greatest country in the free world, is contending with some of the highest homicide rates in the world.

If it is not gun violence, then it is physical violence; if it is not either of these, then it is emotional abuse. We have young brothers who have no respect for life. We have young brothers who hate to be disrespected, disregarded, disagreed with, discarded or just plain dissed. They go to clubs where anything can happen to them. It is not like it was back in the day when people would settle a disagreement with a fight and then move on. No, today, someone has to go their car to retrieve a weapon and often the results are devastatingly permanent. Every day the news headlines are consumed with the aftermath of a culture captivated by and engrossed in violence.

Last year, I attended the Progressive National Baptist Convention and had the opportunity to witness Trayvon Martin's family discuss the "Stand Your Ground" movement, which is a worthwhile campaign—until you become the victim. This culture of violence causes families across America unnecessary pain and heartache. Some of us have experienced the same agony in our own families. It is an ache that is indescribable, because built into the fabric of our lives is the expectation that children will live longer than their parents; not vice versa.

I am trying to paint the image of this text to make it a bit clearer for us to understand. The Bible does not mention how the young man died; however, it does indicate the effects of his death, as I have mentioned. Consider the scene as the family members and professional mourners lay this young man to rest. The saddest part of this event is that his mother is left without any companionship or financial support—she faces a life of complete isolation, a type of social death. Such a lifestyle goes against God's wishes for us. In Genesis, you will find the following words: "…It is not good for man to be alone…" The woman faces a life of potential poverty and misery until one day she herself will be carried to the cemetery, likely in a pauper's grave. Death and Sorrow are rampant in Nain.

But Luke tells us the story of Jesus showing up when He is least expected. The passage reveals to us that Jesus has the uncanny ability to show up when, where and at the time that He is least anticipated. Nain is not a place of great significance; it is outside of a larger city, and yet Jesus showed up there because the grieving woman needed Him.

The torrent of violence in our society against each other has to stop; the abundance of violence by police officers against unarmed young people of color has to stop; the excess of violence against our children has to stop; the frequency of violence against our women has to stop. The only way violence will decrease is if the church reminds the world that there is Good News, even in a culture of violence. The spreading of the Good News begins with Christians modeling non-violent behavior. The old saying is true: "More is caught than is taught." Fathers, if you treat the mother of your children with respect, your sons will learn how to honor and respect women. Mothers, if you treat the father of your children with dignity, your daughters will learn how to do the same to the men in their lives.

I believe that Dr. Martin Luther King Jr's words still ring true today: "It is midnight, our society…" With violence rampant from college campuses, to day care centers, to movie theaters, and schools, "the slaughter of the innocent" must stop; the murder of the virtuous must stop; and the taking of lives before they have a chance to blossom must stop.

I want to remind us that in the midst of all that is going on in the world, the evangelistic church is called to spread the "Good News in a Culture of Violence." I want to present to you the Good News that speaks to a culture of violence that leads to death, and to challenge you to share it with others wherever you go. If we are to evangelize God's people, let's share the Good News of the Gospel of Jesus Christ, which speaks directly to the violence in our culture.

Getting back to the text, Luke's Gospel presents Jesus as a "Peace Maker" – Blessed are the Peace Makers for theirs is the Kingdom of God. The text states that Jesus showed up with His disciples, and a large crowd went to where the grieving mother was. Outside the city gates, one crowd encounters another crowd. One crowd consists of those who are excited to be with Jesus. The other crowd accompanies a woman –whose name we do not have the privilege of knowing – leading people and walking behind her only son who is being carried on a bier to the cemetery, a place that often represents death and demise. But the one thing that cemeteries have that we don't usually consider from our human perspective is potential. This young man dies before his time. Cemeteries are filled with unrealized potential – people who could have been great and never got the opportunity to be.

So as Jesus encounters the woman, he says to her: "Don't cry." Talk about a man who was acquainted with sorrow and knew grief well! This statement demonstrates Jesus' heart reaching out to her. Aren't you glad we serve a God whose heart goes out to us in time of sorrow and distress? Jesus felt what she felt, he hurt like she hurt and He is still doing the same for us today.

One of the subtle points the text is making is that the Lord of Life is speaking directly to Death. Again He says to the weeping mother, "Don't cry." There is probably nothing more emotional than a mother's tears over her dead child. As a Jew, Jesus was versed in the scripture that reads, "Weeping may endure for night but Joy comes in the morning," so it is in this spirit that He tells the woman not to cry. But why would the woman not want to cry out when her world seemed to have been shattered? It's simple: she is in the right place at the right time.

If I could offer some points for you to consider about this text, they would be:

1. **Get in the Right Procession!** Get away from the crowd of Gloom and Doom and position yourself in the crowd of Hope. In the text, one crowd is led by the grieving widow and the other is led by the Lord of Hope. The crowd we choose to surround ourselves with has a profound impact on our ability to cope with difficult and devastating circumstances. Every now and then, it's essential that we change crowds.

   As the story unfolds, Jesus first tells the woman not to cry, and then verse 14 states that He touches the bier. Understand that in that culture for a Rabbi to touch a coffin, he is rendered unclean; he is not supposed to touch the coffin. "When Jesus touches the coffin, according to Jesus' law, he renders Himself unclean from the corruption of the dead boy." (Card, 99) What Jesus shows the people here, and shows us, is that He is capable of performing a paradigm shift of events when we least expect our situations to change. He broke down barriers, for Jesus said, " I didn't come to destroy the law, but to fulfill the law." Jesus demonstrates to us that His compassion for hurting humanity causes Him to forget the rules. But in reality, it is the young man who is given life, and the mother, the widow, is also given her life back—and that is the Good News, both then and now! Here is a woman who is in a procession filled with grief. But she is on a collision course that will change her destiny! This is Good News in a culture of violence.

2. **Then, Get in the Right Position!** Jesus says to the young man, "Get up, because 'The thief "death) comes to steal, kill and to destroy, but I come that you might have life and have it more abundantly.'" (John 10:10). He says that when we collide, this is Good News; in other words, Jesus touched the casket like man but He spoke like God, for next, he said to the young man: "Get Up!" In my Bible, when Jesus says "Get Up!" there is an exclamation point which indicates that what Jesus commands us to do has all power and authority. He speaks to Death itself with great force that only He possesses..

   Verse 15 records that the dead man sat up and began to talk (I wonder what he said!). This story should remind us that when hear God's voice collide with our situations, change must occur. Our faith is restored in Him and in His healing powers. When we hear the Good News we have to do something—we have to get up!

3. **Get Up!** This point represents Life. The Bible says that the young man who had been pronounced dead "sat up and started to talk." However, the

Bible doesn't record what the boy said. Maybe he said something like: "Mama, I'm back!" We don't know for sure, of course, but we do know that he started talking. The passage then says "… and Jesus gave him back to his mother." Whenever you see the word "and," it is a connecting conjunction that connects what was there before to something that will come after it. In other words, what was before was a funeral, full of death and misery. Jesus interrupts the funeral procession and the boy rises up. Can you imagine what the crowd was thinking and saying when Jesus touched the boy? Not only does the boy get up, but he speaks!

When death faces the Creator of Glory, He has to obey! Jesus knew that he had to go to a cross and die, but here he has command over death. Death this is just a precursor to Calvary. But early Easter Sunday morning God said to Death and to the grave, "Let my boy go!" The grave said; "… there is something happening, and I can't hold him." Death said: "I've got to release him now!"

Jesus releases this boy from the grips of Death, and gives him back to his mother. And in verse 16, it is revealed that the people were filled with awe. They were trying to figure out what had happened and realized that they were in the presence of something they could not explain.

When we come to church expecting God to do something, there will be a sense of awe. Worship at its best is a collision between the realities of our lives and the power of God who has the ability to turn our situations around. When our dead dreams meet up with the King of Glory, He has the power to resurrect!

Lastly, the passage states that the people began to praise God because they recognized that there was a great prophet amongst them. And this is a timely word for our situation: in the culture of violence that runs rampant today, the Good News should be spread about Jesus locally, nationally and abroad. Church, when we begin to share our testimony about God—that He is good, that He is great, that He is a healer, that He is a deliverer and that He is a grave-robber—when we share our testimony, that is the Good News! When overcome by life's violent deathlike processions, be encouraged and anticipate the next procession that brings you Hope and Life. Anticipate Victory, Peace and Joy by connecting with the One who has the power to prevail over the encroachment of violence and death and to promote the potential of new life.

References:
Card, Michael. Luke: The Gospel of Amazement. InterVarsity Press, 2011.
New King James Version, The Bible, Luke. 7:11-17.

A RISK OF FAITH
Gina M. Stewart
Mark 5:21-34

Thanks to the persistence of President Obama, the Affordable Health Care is the law of the land, despite the numerous attempts of die-hard opponents desire to repeal it. The ACA has provided health insurance to 12 million Americans through the federal exchange and millions more through Medicaid. Although there is room for improvement, we rejoice that millions of people now have access to healthcare despite pre-existing conditions. But as great as this news may be for some, there are still those, in some states, who will "fall through the cracks."

Workers who earn below $11,670 for single person and up to $46,680 for families cannot afford to purchase the healthcare. The 2010 health law was meant to cover people in these income brackets by expanding Medicaid to workers earning up to the federal poverty line to receive federal subsidies. But in 2012, the Supreme Court struck down the law's requirement that states expand their Medicaid coverage. This meant that states could decide to opt out of expanding Medicaid coverage.

Many elected officials in 24 states, (my state, Tennessee, is one of them) declined the expansion, triggering a coverage gap. Officials said an expansion would add burdensome costs and, in some cases, leave more people dependent on government.

Unfortunately, the decision created a gap for millions of Americans at the lowest income levels who don't qualify for Medicaid coverage under varying state rules. The upshot is that lower-income people in half the states get no help, while better-off workers elsewhere can buy insurance with taxpayer-funded subsidies.

It is a tragic commentary that America is increasingly becoming a place where people "fall through the cracks." The mentally ill "fall through the cracks," the poor "fall the through the cracks," the unemployed and underemployed "fall through the cracks," and women and children "fall through the cracks."

It is not my intent to belittle or bemoan the fact that we live in one of the greatest and richest nations, for which I am grateful to live in a land of such great opportunity. As a matter of fact, I have met people in third world countries who consider America, "The Promised Land." Some of them believe that everyone in America is rich, and, by comparison, that may appear to be so and can be true in many cases; however, the truth is that poverty is still a problem in American.

I am grateful to live in America, and it is a place where dreams can and do come true. Yet, I must say that while the thought of having a chance or an opportunity sounds nice in theory and in recent years has served as the basis for some of the most extreme budget reductions presented on the floor of congress, opportunity does not always take into account that the playing field is not always level. It does not consider the realities of racism, sexism, classism and poverty that lock and shut people out. And when we check statistics, we find that we cannot discuss poverty without including women in the discussion.

According to the Center for American Progress website, Women in America are more likely to be poor than men. Over half of the 37 million Americans living in poverty today are women. And women in America are further behind than women in other countries –the gap in poverty rates between men and women is wider in America than anywhere else in the Western world[1] Consider the following facts:

- Poverty rates are higher for women than men. In 2007, 13.8 percent of females were poor compared to 11.1 percent of men. Women are poorer than men in all racial and ethnic groups.
- Women are poorer than men in all racial and ethnic groups. Black and Latina women face particularly high rates of poverty. Black and Latina women are at least twice as likely as white women to be living in poverty. Only a quarter of all adult women (age 18 and older) with incomes below the poverty line are single mothers. Women are paid less than men, even when they have the same qualifications and work the same hours. And women face a greater risk of poverty.

It can be a terrible thing to be pushed to the margins, ostracized, and disenfranchised, without advocacy, having no one to speak up for you or to lift a voice on your behalf. It can be a terrible thing to be one of those that Dr. Sam Proctor described as being born being behind the scratch line, meaning that just as some of us inherited benefits that we do not deserve, and some have inherited deficits that they do not deserve. It can be a terrible thing to fall through the cracks.

Some of us know what it feels like to fall through the cracks. Some of us know how it feels to be rendered voiceless or invisible because of poverty, gender, race, economic status, age or ethnicity. And, if we have been fortunate to escape these realties, we know of someone who has fallen through the cracks. They are in every family, church, and on every job.

The sister in this text would be in the population who had fallen through the cracks. She would have needed affordable health care, but possibly would not qualify because she was living below the poverty line for the text tells us that all of her money is gone.

She has no name and no identity, like many women in scripture. We know nothing about her or her family tree. Mark provides no information about her marital, economic or social status. We don't know her name, but she is described by her symptoms. She is a woman with a flow of blood, and she has suffered with this "issue" for 12 years. The problem was not that she had a flow of blood, for the flow of blood is normal for women; however, this woman's problem had lasted too long.

And there is nothing like having an issue, a sickness, a problem, a dilemma, a situation or suffering that lasts too long or won't seem to go away. Have you ever faced a situation where it seemed that the more things change the more they remain the same? Have you ever had a problem that lasted too long, a relationship that lasted too long, an assignment that lasted too long, or a hardship that lasted too long? Some may know about those situations where the more things change, the more they remained the same. This woman had a problem that lasted too long. She had been suffering for 12 years.

Twelve years is a long time. It is a long time to be broke, unemployed, caught up in a toxic unproductive relationship, sick, or miserable. Twelve years is a long time to be stuck in the same place, and depending upon the situation and its severity, 12 months, even 12 days can seem like a long time. I have lived through and lived with some situations that have tested my patience, my faith and my resilience because long-term issues have a way of wearing on us. Long-term suffering can take its toll on us. It can leave us feeling powerless and hopeless, void of strength, joy and peace. It can leave us too weak to negotiate the normal responsibilities of life and living.

We cannot be certain what caused this internal hemorrhaging, but we can be certain that she was a very sick woman. Not only did she suffer, but she also lives with the stigma of her disease. Stigma is a powerful and discrediting social label that affects the way individuals view themselves, and the way they are viewed by others. Stigma reduces a person from wholeness to a statistic, to a discounted second-class status. Stigma results in exclusion and isolation as a result of one's status.

The woman lived with the stigma of her disease because she had an issue of blood that had lasted too long. One should not confuse her problem with the regular menstrual cycle which is a normal part of life. Her perpetual bleeding is abnormal which makes her case far more serious.

Continuous bleeding carried major implications for her in those days. Leviticus 15:19-30 contains social and sanitary laws for menstruating women. According to the law, she was considered ceremonially or ritually unclean. Her impurity is transmissible to others until her problem could be rectified. Anyone touching her clothes, chair, bed and the like became ceremonially unclean and anything or anyone she touched became unclean and would be required to bathe and launder their clothing.

The stigma of ritual uncleanness resulted in social contamination. Her condition left her on the fringes of society and excluded her from normal social contact and religious or cultic activity. She needed to be quarantined. She was excluded from temple worship while unclean and could not mingle with crowds in the streets or on the market. In a society where shame and honor were pivotal values, her appearance in public without companions may have indicated "shame status." Because of the nature of her illness, she had been excluded from community and active participation in society for twelve years. She is outside the religious community and the honorable human community.

She lives with a diminished sense of self-worth. She has no one to speak up for her. No father like Jairus to appeal to Jesus in her behalf. She is a nobody. No doubt she has probably been the recipient of all kinds of distorted messages about her value, worth and personhood.

And to make matters even worse, she has spent all of her money, and instead of getting better, she is getting worse. It is quite possible that she would have been counted among the uninsured that would fall between the cracks. The text says that she had spent all her money. Her sickness probably kept her from working. With no job, she has no income, and with no income, she can't pay her bills. She has been drained of her resources and there is no affordable health care.

But I have a sneaky suspicion that this woman must have heard about Jesus of Nazareth, who was administering free health care. Jesus, the Palestian Jew from the hood. Jesus, who was one of the disinherited. Jesus, who went about doing good. I do not know how she heard about him, possibly on FB, or maybe she read a status on Twitter, or saw a picture on Instagram. I do not know how she heard about him, but I have a sneaky suspicion that she must have heard that the common people heard gladly.

Perhaps she heard about how Jesus cast an evil spirit out of a man in the synagogue. Perhaps she heard how he healed Peter's mother-in-law of an excruciating fever, and healed many other sick and demon-possessed people.

I have a sneaky suspicion that she must have heard about how Jesus healed a man with leprosy, a man who was paralyzed, and a man with a withered hand. I have a sneaky suspicion that she must have heard about how Jesus calmed a raging storm and exorcised a legion of demons out of a man who had been living among the tombs. I have a sneaky suspicion that this suffering, sick, stigmatized woman must have heard about what Jesus did for others, and on the basis of his reputation, she decided to seek his help.

I believe that on the basis of the reports she had heard concerning Jesus, she was convinced that if he could heal leprosy and fevers, cast out devils, and calm the tempest, then surely he could make her whole.

That is probably how she ended up in the crowd on that day. Her very life depended upon her getting to Jesus. Have you been in a situation where your very life depended on you getting to Jesus? For life is in the Blood.

Leviticus 17:11 states that we must have enough blood flowing around our body or else our bodily functions deteriorate and we die.

Blood is fundamental to the function of every cell of every component in our bodies. Cells need food to survive, grow, repair themselves, fulfill their specific functions, and to reproduce. Cellular food is transported in blood to provide energy for all the cells needs. We are multicellular organisms, having separate specialized organs with highly sophisticated functions. Transport and communication between these structures is essential.

This woman had been bleeding 12 years! Her very life depended on getting to Jesus! But there is a slight problem, she is in the crowd with Jesus but she is not on his itinerary. Jesus is on his way to the home of Jairus, the desperate ruler of the Synagogue, to heal his 12-year-old daughter who is at the point of death.

On the surface, Jairus seems to have the advantage. He is male, ritually pure, and holds a religious office. The woman on the other hand is unnamed, female, impure, impoverished and destitute.

But notice that despite everything that is working against her – stigma, status, and sickness – she refuses to resign herself to live like this forever. Despite her stigma, her status and her sickness she refused to accept her issue as permanent.

There are people who have accepted the report that your issue is permanent; that this is as good as it gets; that your best days are behind you; and that the odds are stacked against you. The enemy of our souls tries to use what looks like hopeless situations to exploit our faith and convince that it is our destiny to live like this and that you may as well resign yourself to an unprofitable destiny.

Sometimes, it can be very tempting to resign. Resign from life; resign from the faith; resign from believing that you still have hope and a future. Sometimes, life is like a game of Words with Friends or a bad hand of Spades, where it seems that there is no way you can win with the hand you have been dealt.

Thank God that this woman resolves – *resolve: to decide firmly on a course of action. Firm determination to do something.* In other words, it means to make up in your mind to do whatever it takes. Rutgers' paralyzed football player Eric LaGrand resolved that he would graduate from college despite his injury. He told the crowd at his commencement, "Don't ever let someone tell you that you can't do something." Gabby Douglas resolved that she would be an Olympic champion. Nehemiah resolved that he would rebuild Jerusalem's walls despite the opposition of Sanballat and Tobias. David resolved that he would slay Goliath in spite of his size. And the woman with the issue of Blood refused to resign herself to an unprofitable destiny. She resolved that she couldn't live the rest of her life like this; she resolved that whatever it takes she's going to reach out and touch Jesus. She believed that Jesus' touch had power. She takes a risk of faith, and the risk paid off.

Every now and then, we have to talk to ourselves like that woman and refuse to accept our issues as permanent. Every now and then, we have to be desperate enough to break the rules and declare, "Whatever it takes, I'm going to touch Jesus."

This woman was desperate enough to break the rules, because she is determined to touch Jesus. Even though she did not have an appointment; even though she was just a face in the thronging crowd; even though Jesus was headed to heal Jairus' 12-year-old daughter; the Bible says that when she heard of Jesus, she came up behind him in the press and said, "If I can but touch the hem of his garment, I shall be made whole."

Some of us, if not all of us, have been behind in a lot of things. We have been behind in our dreams, in our resolutions, in our finances, in our goals, and in our spiritual growth. But there comes a time when we have to do what that woman with the flow of blood did, and take a risk of faith.

A few of you may be in stressful situations, and you were just about to resign. You were about to resign from life, resign from the faith, and resign from believing that you still have hope and a future. But this is for the folks with the "whatever it takes faith." In spite of what the situation looks, you *resolve* to do what the woman with the issue of blood did. "I am going to take the risk." "I am going to reach out and touch Jesus." If Jesus could heal that woman with the issue of blood, if Jesus could give sight to the blind, if Jesus can unstop deaf ears, if Jesus can raise Lazarus from the dead, if Jesus can feed a multitude with two fish and five loaves of bread, then surely, Jesus can turn your situation around.

I may be coming up from behind, but I am going to go for it! I am going for my healing, for my deliverance, and for my breakthrough. Today, I will take my life back because the same Jesus who healed that woman is the same Jesus who can turn my situation around, heal my body, deliver my children, save my marriage, and restore my finances.

I refuse to die like this. I cannot die sick. I cannot die broke. I cannot die frustrated. I cannot die depressed. I'm going to take the risk!

Notes
[1]*www.wmich.edu/hhs/newsletter_journals/jssw/32-2.htm*

Standing Firm In Critical Times: Our God Is Able
Kenneth J. Flowers
Daniel 3:16-18

As the 30th Annual Session of the Michigan Progressive Baptist Convention comes to a close, we conclude by putting our emphasis on "Missions," which is the crux of our faith. For true "Missions" really is translating the Gospel of Jesus Christ from a story in the Bible into concrete, practical experiences which touch human lives and transform human hearts. When one is able to hear the Word of God, accept it, believe it and receive it, and then engage in living the Word, one is truly practicing missions. And this is what our Convention must do: Understand the mission of the church and put it into practice, which in theological terms is called *praxis*.

The mission of the church is to preach the Gospel of Jesus Christ, *first and foremost*, which denotes the *spiritual*, and to also address the political, economic and social conditions of society which dehumanize the person and demoralize the spirit. Too much focus on either one and not enough focus on the other will result in a major imbalance, which in turn will create either religious fanatics who are "so heavenly bound that they are no earthly good," or political, economic & social dysfunctionates" who have no spiritual & moral parameters to govern their lives. There must be balance; but there also must be transformation of hearts and the dedication of lives if we are to really move forward and honor God and praise His name.

In our text for tonight, we hear a familiar story about three Hebrew boys -- young, if you will – Shadrach, Meshach and Abednego. These young men were so committed and dedicated to the Lord that they refused to follow the king of Babylon. Even though King Nebuchadnezzar had found favor upon these three young Hebrews and had appointed them administrators over the province of Babylon at Daniel's urging, Shadrach, Meshach and Abednego would not follow the King's decree. Why? Because they knew who they were, and such knowledge enabled them to also know whose the were. You see the names "Shadrach", "Meshach" and "Abednego" were actually Babylonian names given to them by the chief official after they had been taken into Babylonian captivity. Their Hebrew names, which were their birth names, were Hananiah, Mishael and Azariah. And being Hebrew from birth, they were steeped in Jewish culture and also the holy tenets of Judaism. They knew the Ten Commandments backwards and forward because they were "Israelites from the royal family and the nobility. [They were] young men without any physical defect, handsome, showing aptitude from every kind of learning, well informed, quick to understand, and qualified to serve in the king's palace" (Daniel 1:3-4). They were extraordinary individuals who the king thought were just right to serve him. Nebuchadnezzar thought, "These young men will serve me honorably and do what I say and keep the people in line." But the king evidently did not know much about Judaism because if he had known the devotion, commitment and dedication of the Hebrews to "love the Lord thy God with all thine heart, and with all thy soul and with all thine might" (Deuteronomy 6:5), and to "have no other gods before me," (Exodus 20:3), he would not have made the request that he made. Moreover, had he fully realized and believed in the power of Yaheveh, he would not have put the Lord to the test. We ought not put God to the test, FOR GOD IS SOVEREIGN!!!

Well, what exactly is the request of King Nebuchadnezzar and how does he put the Lord our God to the test? Well, it's right there in the text. Daniel, Chapter 3 says that King Nebuchadnezzar made an image of gold 90 feet high and 9 feet wide and set it up on the plain of Dura in the province of Babylon. He then summoned all the officials --- the satraps, prefects, governors, advisers, treasurers, judges, magistrates, and all other provincial officials (which included Shadrach, Meshach and Abednego) to come for the dedication ceremonies. They were commanded that as soon as they heard the sound of music--- the sound of the horn, flute, zither, lyre, harp, pipes and all kinds of music, They *must* falldown and worship the image of gold that Nebuchadnezzar had set up. Whoever did not fall down and worship the image of gold would immediately be thrown into a blazing furnace.

When the music began, all the peoples, nations and men of every language fell down and worshipped the image of gold that King Nebuchadnezzar had built – that is everyone EXCEPT Shadrach, Meshach and Abednego! They refused to bow down and worship a false god.

Some astrologers came forth and denounced the Jews. They told the King that these three Hebrew young men would not bow down. They said, "But there are some Jews whom you have set over the affairs of the province of Babylon – Shadrach, Meshach and Abednego – who pay no attention to you, Your Majesty. They neither serve your gods nor worship the image of gold you have set up" (Daniel 3:12). The king was more than angry! He could not believe that the very ones he trusted – Shadrach, Meshach and Abednego – would turn on him and NOT follow his decree!!!

"Furious with rage, Nebuchadnezzar summoned Shadrach, Meshach and Abednego. So these men were brought before the king, and Nebuchadnezzar said to them, 'Is it true, Shadrach, Meshach and Abednego, that you do not serve my gods or worship the image of gold I have set up? Now when you hear the sound of the horn, flute, zither, lyre, harp, pipe and all kinds of music, if you are ready to fall down and worship the image I made, very good. But if you do not worship it, you will be thrown immediately into a blazing furnace. Then what god will be able to rescue you from my hand?'" (Daniel 3:13-15)

But Shadrach, Meshach and Abednego refused to be intimidated by the king's threat. When you are a man or a woman of principle, there ought not be any position or title on earth that will make you compromise your principles nor negotiate your integrity! Never be beholden to politicians, rulers of this carnal world, nor anyone else who does not have the power to save your soul from eternal damnation! Rather, only trust God, and Him only must we serve!!!

"Shadrach, Meshach & Abednego replied to him, 'King Nebuchadnezzar, we do not need to defend ourselves before you in this matter. If we are thrown into the blazing furnace, the God we serve is able to deliver us from it, and He will deliver us from your hand, O king. But even if He does not, we want you to know, O king, that we will not serve your gods or worship the image of gold you have set up.'" (Daniel 3:16-18).

They displayed righteous indignation and reminded Nebuchadnezzar that our God is able to rescue us even from the hand of the enemy!!! But even in His own Sovereign will, if He chooses not to deliver us, our faith will not be diminished, neither will our hope be lost. For our faith and dedication is to the God of Abraham, Isaac and Jacob. If He says "No" to us, we will praise Him ANYHOW!!! But we will not serve your gods nor worship your image of gold.

When King Nebuchadnezzar heard this bold and courageous statement from Shadrach, Meshach and Abednego, he was even more furious and ordered the furnace heated seven times hotter than usual. "The temperature was controlled by the number of bellows forcing air into the fire chamber. Therefore, sevenfold intensification was achieved by seven bellows pumping at the same time. But the expression 'seven times hotter than usual' may have been figurative for as hot as possible' since seven signifies completeness.' (NIV Study Bible). In any event, the furnace was as hot as it could get!

Some of the strongest soldiers were gotten to take Shadrach, Meshach and Abednego to the fiery furnace. They were bound and were wearing their robes, trousers, turbans and other clothes. They were thrown into the furnace, firmly tied, hands and feet. The flames were so hot that the soldiers were killed by the fire.

"Then King Nebuchadnezzar leaped to his feet in amazement and asked his advisers, 'Weren't there three men that we tied up and threw into the fire?' They replied, 'Certainly, O king.' He said, 'Look! I see four men walking around in the fire, unbound and unharmed, and the fourth looks like the Son of God.'" Nebuchadnezzar then summoned Shadrach, Meshach and Abednego to come out of the fiery furnace. So they "came out of the fire and all of the satraps, prefects, governors and royal advisers crowded around them. They saw that the fire had not harmed their bodies, nor was a hair of their heads singed; their robes were not scorched, and there was no smell of fire on them. Then Nebuchadnezzar said, 'Praise be to the God of Shadrach, Meshach and Abednego, who has sent His angel and rescued His servants! They trusted in Him and defied the king's command and were willing to give up their lives rather than serve or worship any god except their own God. Therefore I decree that the people of any nation or language who say anything against the God of Shadrach, Meshach and Abednego be cut into pieces and their houses be turned into piles of rubble, for no other god can save in this way.' Then the king promoted Shadrach, Meshach and Abednego in the province of Babylon" (Daniel 3:26-30).

You may ask, "What is the point of the story. The point is *do not bow down to the gods of this world, but stand firm in the Lord!* Earlier, I told you the true Hebrew names of Shadrach, Meshach & Abednego. I researched and further understand why they would not bow down.

Shadrach would not bow down because his Hebrew name was *Hananiah* – "The Lord Shows Grace" – He believed in his heart that the Lord would show him grace and mercy because of God's unmerited favor towards him. *"Amazing Grace, how sweet the sound that saved a wretch like me! I once was lost, but now I'm found, was blind but now I see. Through many dangers, toils and snares, I've already come; 'tis Grace hath brought me safe thus far, and grace will lead me home."*

Meshach would not bow down because his Hebrew name was Mishael – "Who is what God is?" In other words, he believed that God is God all by Himself. God says, "I am that I am" so Meshach believed God would be a Deliverer from the fiery furnace and deliver him. So he refused to bow down, but trusted in God!!!

Abednego would not bow down because his Hebrew name was Azariah – "The Lord helps" – and he believed that the Lord would help him in his hour of trouble. He believed that "The Lord Will Make a Way Somehow!" He believed, *"The Lord is my light and my salvation, whom shall I fear? The Lord is the strength of my life, of whom shall I be afraid?"* (Psalm 27:1).

So I say to you:

- Don't bow down to the gods of drugs, sex, money, jealousy, envy, gossip, corruption, and cynicism!
- Don't bow to the god of "Doing it my way!"
- Don't bow to the god of "Not following Leadership"
- Stand firm in Christ Jesus!
- Stand firm, knowing "the Lord will make a way!"
- Stand firm, like a tree planted by the river of water!
- Stand firm, for "I'm pressing on the upward way, new heights I'm gaining every day, still praying as I onward bound, Lord plant my feet on Higher Ground!"

DON'T GIVE UP ON JESUS
Willie R. Davis
John 11: 1-4, 17-27, 28-33

Walk with me...

Lazarus of Bethany, also known as Saint Lazarus or Lazarus of the Four Days, which is also referenced as *The City of the Siblings*, Mary, Martha and Lazarus. The place where Jesus lodged. Some believe that the present village of Bethany does not occupy the site of the ancient village, but that it grew up around the traditional cave which they propose to have been at some distance from the house of Martha and Mary in the village. There are others who have concluded that ancient Bethany was the site of an almshouse for the poor and a place of care for the sick.

There are hints of association between Bethany and care of the unwell in the Gospel – Mark's gospel tells of Simon the Leper's house (Mk 14:3-10). Jesus receives urgent word of Lazarus' illness here from Bethany. As we walk into the scene of the life of this Lazarus, let's keep in mind the main incidents surrounding this Bethany...

1. Raising of Lazarus from the dead.
2. The entry of Jesus into Jerusalem on Palm Sunday was near Bethany
3. The lodging place following this week in Bethany (Matt 21:17, Mk 11:11,12)
4. The dinner in the house of Simon the Leper at which Mary anoints Jesus
5. Before the Ascension of Jesus into heaven

Now the place is in question today...as most things that are related to Christ and Christians, as to why we should not "Give Up On Jesus."

Now, concerning us – you and me – if the question were asked it would be, how did we get HERE? This place, at this time, and for what reason, why here and why now?

There are critical facts to our relationship to Christ and the church today that concerns me, and, it should concern you, under the banner of "Don't Give Up On Jesus." As a matter of fact there are seven, produced by one church research organization called "Church Leaders."

1. Less than 20% of Americans regularly attend church, one half of what previous pollsters reported for the past 70 years.
2. In 2004, one study number showed that in the Orthodox Christian Church/Catholic mainline and Evangelical only 17.7% regularly attend church.
3. Over the past 30 to 40 years, most denominations have reported a decline in church attendance.
4. One group, who authored the "National Congregation Study," calls it the halo effect – meaning the difference between what people say, and what they actually do.

Another research, surveying the growth of U.S. Protestants discovered that the majority of people don't belong to a local church; yet, they identify with church roots, on the heels of the fact that they attend church less than 12 times a year and that number reflects about 78 million.

5. American church is steadily declining.
6. Only one state is outpacing its population growth and that is Hawaii.
7. American churches as a whole did not keep up with population growth from 1994-2014.

"Don't Give Up On Jesus"

The researchers conclude that churches from 40-190 years old are declining and increase in churches are only 1/4 of whats needed to keep up with population growth. The researchers indicate that in 2050 the percentage of US population attending church will be almost half of what it was in 1990. The National Poll on Americans Priorities of concerns facing our country was nine.... religious values and prayer was number eight.

- Economy, Jobs 20%
- Misc Social Issues 7%
- Racism, Race Relation 5%
- Misc Government Issues 4%
- Income Gap/Disparity 4%
- Immigration, Illegal Immigrants 3%
- President Barack Obama 3%
- Religious Values & Prayer 3%
- Police Problems, Corruption 3%

"Don't Give Up On Jesus"

Which brings us to the subject of people Lazarus, Martha, and Mary, place Bethany, and this Death. In this life no matter the consequences or circumstances of we should never *Give Up On Jesus*!

Our first point of emphasis of distraction is FRIEND... the message sent from the sisters to "He Whom You Love". Verses 3,5,7,11... We can never allow our friendships with others to distract us from the presence or question His power. Yes Jesus was their friend, to Lazarus, Martha and Mary, but it didn't conflict with his mission where he was. We should never let FRIEND or FRIENDSHIP put a time on our relationship to Him.

Our second point of emphasis is FAMILY.... As Jesus approached Bethany it was clear that family Martha, Mary and others were gather in the house of hopelessness and grief concerning Lazarus death. Interestingly Martha was the one in the family who first ran to Jesus with a little gleam of confidence in Jesus....as we all should do in the time of all consequences and circumstances. Martha did question the presence and the power by saying "If you had been here" limiting the presence and power of Jesus to be everywhere at all times with all power....He is Omnipotence, Omnipresence, and Omniscience..... but Martha did have hope, "but even now I know that whatever You ask of God, God will give You". Verses 20-23;32,33 Mary on the other hand stayed in the house of hopelessness and grief. When she was secretly summoned by Martha that Jesus called for her then and only then did she move. Mary who had anointed Jesus before in the same house, only when she came and saw Him she also replied "Lord if You had been here". There are times when FAMILY fails the test of Giving Up On Jesus...!!!

Thirdly and finally the last point of emphasis is FAITH...... Jesus did what He always does, take command by commanding, Faith comes by hearing, hearing by the word of God..He spoke "Take away the stone.... when our actions displays FAITH it will override FRIENDS AND FAMILY. Without FAITH it is impossible to please God, but with FAITH we can do all things. When we act in Faith for our Families we can convert our Friends also, Don't Give Up On Jesus!!!

When we Don't Give Up On Jesus....we can move the stones of our lives that block the exits of our conditions, circumstances and consequences..... They had compassion but they didn't have connections, they had man power but they didn't have all power, they put Lazarus in the cave but they couldn't call Lazarus out of the grave, they buried him but they could not resurrect him. You can't *Give Up On Jesus!*

When friends and family cried out, Lazarus stayed lying down, when Jesus cried out "Lazarus come forth" he got up. *Don't Give Up On Jesus!*

"Loose him and let him go" Jesus freed us all at Calvary, just as he did Lazarus at Bethany. After conquering the suffering of the cross, death and the grave, Jesus did as he said to Martha "I am the Resurrection and the Life, He who believes in Me, though he may die, he shall live. *Don't Give Up On Jesus!*

Jesus is not just our hope for now, he is our last and only hope for now and the future, we can't Give Up On Jesus. We need him brother and sisters to help us wait for his arrival and directions. He didn't do this just for the Lazarus family he did for Lazarus' friends and his disciples. He did it for us, so that we could believe in Him in life and the Resurrection.

When Jesus arrives in our lives, he addresses our sick conditions which can put us in the grave. As was Lazarus' sickness was not unto death, but for the glory of God. There is no condition that can't be changed by Jesus to give God glory. We cannot *Give Up On Jesus* when we know that all of Bethany was suffering from sick conditions and it was time for the glory of God to appear.

Once Jesus arrives into our lives just as he did in Bethany he can change our dead circumstances. Let it be known that the reason for Lazarus' sickness was never discussed and the reason never known. As a matter of fact, Lazarus is the only identified person in the Gospel whose name follows the word "certain." Usually they never indicate a name, because "certain" was good enough.

This was not just a Lazarus sick condition and dead circumstance; it was for Bethany's sake to see the consequences of the Glory of God. We cannot *Give Up On God!*

BORN TO DO IT
Jacqueline A. Thompson
James 1:22-25

I had the wonderful experience of having breakfast with the wife of the 44th President of the United States – the first during Black History Month. As I sat and reflected in the awe of that moment, in the awe of that Black African-American First Lady – Mrs. Michelle LaVaughn Robinson Obama. In awe of what people had to endure to arrive at the place where an African American couple occupied the highest office in the land, I could not help but wonder where we would be, as a people, if our foremothers and forefathers had been hearers only and not doers. What if we were descendants of a people who heard the word of God but had no desire to act upon it? There would have been no Underground Railroad; no Emancipation Proclamation; no National Association for the Advancement of Colored People; no Sojourner Truth; no Booker T. Washington and Tuskegee University; no W.E.B. DuBois and ***The Souls of Black Folk***; no *Brown vs. the Board of Education*, no Thurgood Marshall; no Civil Rights Act. What if we had come from a people that were hearers only? There would have been no Harlem Renaissance. Had Louis Armstrong only been a hearer, how would we see trees of green and red roses too? How would we know they are blooming for me and blooming for you? We wouldn't think to ourselves, *What a Wonderful World!* Had Langston Hughes only been a hearer, how would the world ever know that *life for us ain't been no crystal stair?* What if Maya Angelou had only been a hearer, how would we know *Why the Caged Birds Sing?* We have descended from a people that were not just hearers but doers!

There are those who wonder why we continue to focus on our history. They believe there is no need. But it is our history, recalling where we have been in the past that gives us context for where we are in the present and serves as inspiration for where we are trying to go in the future, We learn lessons from where we have been that helps us understand where we are, so that we can get to where we need to go. Had Sojourner Truth not stood for justice as a black woman, Shirley Chisolm may not have stood as the first black woman to run for president, and Congresswoman Barbara Lee may not have stood as the only person to vote against the Iraq war, a war we are still fighting today. It was the VISION of a better world that Frederick Douglass held that paved the way for the DREAM of Martin Luther King, Jr. that made it possible for then Senator Barack Obama to be the CHANGE somebody could believe in. All of this was made possible, because they were not just hearers but doers.

In light of our rich legacy, too voluminous to recount in this moment, who are we – in these times – to think it is okay to fade into the background of history? Who are we to accept the status quo? Who are we to let reality television be the entire definition of us? We are more than statistics. We are more than a HIV/AIDS rate. We are more than a homicide rate. We are more than what is reflected in our prison population. Who are we to think that is okay to be content in not doing what God called us to do? We descended from a people who had nothing to hold onto but a word, a promise, a hope and a dream but they believed that word and they acted.

We do not have to look to history alone. Even in our personal lives, we have countless figures that will never make the history books, but their faith, prayers and actions have paved the way for where many of us sit today. None of us have made it alone. We are sitting on the backs and standing on the shoulders of those who came before us. We do not have to accept the picture that the news and other media paint of us and our children. If our ancestors could break the back of slavery, surely we can save the countless young men and women left to the streets. If they could build an Underground Railroad, surely we can find a way to end human trafficking. Without formal education, degrees, financial resources and the trappings of materialism, there were 173 Black inventions recorded before Blacks were legally allowed to invent anything. There are those who would suggest they did more with less, and we are doing less with so much more. We do not have a right to rest on our laurels and legacy being hearers only, having descended from a people who did so much.

It makes sense that they would be doers. As a people of faith, created in the image and likeness of God, they would be doers. They believed in and served a God that not hears but does. It is the doing nature of God that makes prayer so powerful. When we pray, it is not just that God hears us but we believe God will do something about what we have prayed about. If you have ever been healed; ever been blessed; ever been delivered; ever been provided for; ever been protected; ever prayed and God answered, then you can testify that God not only hears but will answer. It would be enough if God just heard and answered, but while God is answering our prayers – God is still simultaneously causing the Sun to rise in the East and set in the West. God is still causing the Sun to give light by day and Moon to light the night. God is still keeping oceans and seas from overflowing their banks. While hearing and answering prayer, God is still sustaining the world by God's Will. If that was all God did, that would be enough. But God in God's infinite greatness does all of that, all while doing great things for us. Still waking us up; still keeping us in our right minds; still opening doors; and still confounding our enemies. God is a God that does and not just hears.

Yet we know we have an enemy whose assignment it is to keep us from doing what we know we have heard God tell us to do. Often God will tell us to do things that most of us do not really want to do. I don't mind loving, but why must I love my enemies? Do I have to bless those that curse me? Do I really have to pray for those who spitefully use me? Must I really forgive them, believing that they know not what they do – when I know many of them know exactly what they are doing? God often requires us to do the very things that we do not want to do. Even Jesus, the Son of the Living God struggled with what God, the Father expected him to do. In the Garden of Gethsemane, Jesus asked God to let this cup pass from him but knowing God's plan and purpose was what mattered, surrendered saying, "Nevertheless, not my will but thine be done."

The generations that came before us were doers, not for their own benefit but to benefit those of us that would come behind them. So we must ask ourselves, what are we willing to do? What are we willing to do to benefit someone else? What are we willing to do for those who are on their way and will come behind us? How will we overcome the enemy who does all he can to keep us from doing what God has purposed and planned? We were born to have impact. We were created to perform great and mighty acts. We have all we need to deal with ills that plague our community. The solutions to the injustices, inequities, and divisions that exist in our communities lie within us. Are we willing to make the sacrifices, take the risks, and *be doers and not hearers only?* This text speaks to us and instructs us on how to *be doers and not hearers only.* The author is writing to Jewish Christians who have been scattered abroad because of persecution. Not general persecution but a very specific persecution, where the poor were being exploited and oppressed by the wealthy. The wealthy landowners instituted practices and laws that created an entire class of working poor. It is the same persecution many in this nation and our world experience today. We debated raising the minimum wage. We debated whether or not all people should have access to basic and affordable healthcare. We are still debating if people should be provided a path to citizenship. Truly, there is nothing new under the sun!

As a prelude to our text, James begins his writing by instructing the people to take a stance that appears completely antithetical to their experience. In James 1:2, he says to "Count it all joy, my brothers, when you meet trials of various kinds..." His instruction completely messed me up. This is not a joyful circumstance for the people to be experiencing. But one thing I have learned from those nameless, faceless Black History heroes and sheroes. They knew how to exercise their faith and they knew how to defeat the enemy. Many of us remained trapped and ensnared by the enemy because when we experience trials of various kinds, we broadcast it. We post it on Facebook and send it by email. We repeat the experience incessantly to all who will listen. It shows on our faces and affects our moods and countenance. But our ancestors understood what James was trying to communicate. They knew the power of finding joy in every situation. Joy is not produced by circumstances. Joy helps us transcend circumstances. The prophet Nehemiah reminds us in chapter 8, verse 10 that the "joy of the Lord is our strength." James needed the hearers of this epistle to know that just because the situation is not good, God is still good and the goodness of God will prevail. The goodness of God will cause all things to work together for their good.

James then goes on to admonish them with the words of our text: *Be doers of the word and not hearers only.* To be hearers of the Word only is to be like a man who must constantly look in the mirror to remember what he looks like. As a people, we have become like that man. In many ways, we are a people who have forgotten what we look like. We have forgotten where we have come from and from Whom we came. Present-day culture, as seen in music, literature, movies, media and even news would lead one to believe that we are a people consumed with self-gratification and physical satiation by any means necessary. Our daughters are referred to as "hoes" and our sons as "thugs," Our mothers, sisters, and aunts as abusers and manipulators of the system and our fathers, brothers, and uncles as absent, either by death, desertion, or prison. But the Word of God is clear, it is not about who we are or where we come from. Unfortunately, many of us have succumbed to these images constantly set before us; so much so that we now see and define each other in the negative ways that others have historically defined us. But James comes to speak to us about how we can become the doers, serving our generation and fulfilling God's purpose in our time.

James says if we want to be doers of the word, we must first *get intently focused on the right thing*. We are living during a time where the competition for our attention is intense. It is easy to be distracted by the things we must do; by things we want to do and by the things we avoid doing. If we are not careful, we will find ourselves in constant pursuit of and in bondage to things that don't really matter and can never really satisfy. It is only when we are facing trials and tribulations that we discover where our focus has really been.

He says to *look into the perfect law of liberty*. Scholars throughout history have debated and contemplated about "what" is the perfect law of liberty. Some suggest the perfect law of liberty refers to the Decalogue. Others purport that the perfect law of liberty refers to a universal law. I suggest to you the perfect law of liberty is not just a what, but a who. The only way we can be doers of God's Word is through a personal living, dynamic relationship with Jesus Christ. Jesus is the fulfillment of the law. We cannot accomplish what God has called us to do individually or corporately without the sustained presence and power of Jesus Christ. It is in Him that we live and move and have our being. It requires us to be rooted and grounded. It requires us to remain consistently connected to the one who came to set us free. It is this liberty found in the redemptive work of Christ that frees us to do what God is calling us to do in the world. When we keep our focus on the source of our strength, we are empowered to all that God has created us to do. Everything we need to do, we can do – and will do through Christ who gives us strength.

James goes on to say that in addition to being intently focused on the right thing, to be doer – *we must remember what we have heard*. God is always speaking. It is critical that we are a people, who remembers what God has said and does it. "Do not forget" is the admonition repeated continuously to the Israelites as they were being delivered from bondage and being brought into the Promised Land. Their ability to remember and their ability to shape the memory of the next generation would be critical to their success physically and spiritually. They are told to remember their history of bondage. They are told to remember God's deliverance. They are told to remember God's instruction and statutes and to obey them. They are told quite simply to not forget the Lord their God. James echoes that sentiment for us today through this text. Our memory is critically connected ability to be doers of God's word. It is vital to achieving the purposes and plans of God. Paul, in Romans 10:17, underscores this truth by declaring, "Faith comes from what is heard, and what is heard comes through the preached word of Christ." God has said some things to encourage us, to empower us, to strengthen us, to correct us, to guide us and to instruct us. God has done some things for us that assure us of God's faithfulness when we are unsure. We must be willing to let the refrain of this hymn become our prayer:

> *Lest I forget Gethsemane;*
> *Lest I forget thy agony;*
> *Lest I forget thy love for me;*
> *Lead me to Calvary*

Finally, James assures the people that there is no need to be concerned about success in their endeavors. Their actions will not be in vain. If they are faithful and consistent in their obedience, *God will bless them in their doing.* The blessing is in obedience to the Word. I am reminded of the many times Jesus was on his way to Jerusalem traveling between Samaria and Galilee. He enters a village and encounters ten lepers. They stood at a distance crying out to Jesus for mercy. Jesus simply told them to go and show themselves to the priest. He did not lay his hands on them. He did not command the leprosy to leave their bodies or pronounce healing. He did not even pray. He gave an instruction. There was no immediate healing like for woman with the issue of blood. There was no instant manifestation or proof that change had occurred at all like with Blind Bartimaeus or the paralytic man. This healing required action on their part. It required them to be obedient and be doers of the Word of the Lord. The Bible says, *as they went – they were healed.* They were blessed as they were doing.

This is how it will be for us. We are not living at a time where we can rest on our historical accomplishments and achievements. There is still much work to be done. Racism and injustice still plague us. Sexism and gender bias still exist within and outside our community. Health and economic disparities continue to widen, clearly defining the haves and the have nots. Our families, seniors, and children are still the most vulnerable in our communities and often are the target of legislation that undermines their security. God's instruction is clear:

For I was hungry and you gave me food, I was thirsty and you gave me drink, I was a stranger and you welcomed me, I was naked and you clothed me, I was sick and you visited me, I was in prison and you came to me.' Then the righteous will answer him, saying, 'Lord, when did we see you hungry and feed you, or thirsty and give you drink? And when did we see you a stranger and welcome you, or naked and clothe you? And when did we see you sick or in prison and visit you?' And the King will answer them, 'Truly, I say to you, as you did it to one of the least of these my brothers, you did it to me. Matthew 25:35-40

The words of Dr. Martin Luther King Jr. also remind us of our responsibility.

We must come to see that human progress never rolls in on wheels of inevitability. It comes through the tireless efforts and persistent work of men willing to be co-workers with God, and without this hard work time itself becomes an ally of the forces of social stagnation. We must use time creatively, and forever realize that the time is always ripe to do right. Letter from Birmingham Jail, 1963

We know what is required of us. We must make the decision to just do it, knowing that God will bless us as we are doing it. Change wasn't immediate for the ones that came before us. Like the heroes of faith found in Hebrews 11, they died in faith having never seen the fruits of their labor or the promise fulfilled. But they acted in faith believing that change would come. We are the beneficiaries of their doing. We are here because God blessed them in their doing. We owe them and the generations that will follow. We were born to serve our generation in our time believing that the same God who brought us this far, will be with us the rest of the way. We've come this far by faith; Leaning on the Lord! Trusting in His Holy Word, He's never failed us yet. We can't turnaround now. We've come this far by faith.

The Encouragement of Adversity
Charlie Dates
Philippians 1:12-18

In 1897, as he was sitting in his living room reading the New York Journal, he came across his own obituary. It was strange because he was alive and reading his own obituary. It turns out that the editors of the New York Journal received the news that his cousin – James Ross Clemens passed away. Without verifying the information, the New York Journal eagerly printed the obituary for Samuel Longhorn Clemens. We know him by his pen name Mark Twain. It is at that point when Mark Twain writes to the New York Journal these famous words: "The news of my demise has been greatly exaggerated."

Life has a way of exaggerating the details of your circumstances. If you're not careful you too will believe the hyperbole about your own life.

That seems to be the tenor and tone with which the aged apostle Paul is writing to the upstart church in Philippi. Concerned about his welfare and knowing that he is personally financing his Roman imprisonment, the church – beloved of their pastor and demonstrating their concern for him – sends him a financial gift through Epaphroditus. In response, Paul writes them a short thank you note; an epistle we call Philippians.

It is as though he is saying – out the gate, immediately after his customary salutation – that they ought not believe reports that his circumstances are bringing about the demise of his ministry and his life. Quite to the contrary, Paul writes the Philippians the startling words of our text: it turns out that his circumstances are working for the progress of his ministry and for the furtherance of the gospel of Jesus Christ.

That's startling for 2 reasons:

1. Paul's physical location
2. The joy with which he intentionally pens this epistle.

So many of us read through that too quickly. Feel the force of the mutually exclusive nature of those two startling reasons.

He is in jail on his own dime. It's bad enough to be in jail. It's worse to have to pay for your own stint. See him with your mind's eye. Paul sits in a plush Roman apartment chained to a rotating guard. He is unable to work, to leave at will, to dine alfresco at the local Gellato eatery. Yet, he writes to this Philippian church with a strange dominating theme. He uses the word *joy* more than 12 times in this four Chapter epistle. It is the word chairoo – the word from which we get our English word charismatic – a joy-filled person. It is as though the theme of joy is dripping from his pen in every paragraph.

Now I can tell you with a fair measure of confidence that if I were in jail with the opportunity to write my church in Chicago, my letter would be brief and to the point. It would be about five words long: GET ME OUT OF HERE. Don't get me wrong, I appreciate prison ministry, just not enough to stay there when the ministry is done.

Not so with the aged, godly apostle. Not only is he not asking for legal reprieve, but he is also saying that this jail stint is working out, falling out, turning out for the good of his ministry. As a result, he has decided to rejoice and in the face of the unknown future to keep on rejoicing.

Do you get the point? Do you see the picture?

This text is tailored to teach us that you can have real joy in unlikely circumstances when the motivation for your joy is not your circumstances.

The repetitive emphasis on joy in this epistle borders on the improbable for its resilient optimism in the face of very difficult circumstances. But I want to caution us against reading this passage as religious feel good fluff. This is not obnoxious optimism. This is not philosophical detachment from reality; but rather this is principled expectation in the providence of God.

This passage does not ask of us mindless dismissal of real life circumstances. Instead it pushes upon us a heavenly analysis for Christian endurance.

How does this text cause us to view the work of God in our difficult circumstances? How can we have joy in unlikely circumstances?

Circumstances are catalysts not constraints.

Paul argues that the circumstances of every believer are catalysts, not constraints. Verse 12 opens with a verbal construction that begets epistemological certainty. The Philippian church can have confident assurance that Paul's circumstances are beneficial. This is important because Paul rarely delves into his personal circumstances so early in his letters. There is a discernable, palpable affection shared between the Philippian church and him. Even the end of the epistle acknowledges their unusual and generous support of Paul's ministry. He cares for them and they care for him. Oh to God that such a joyous exchange were not so rare between pulpit and pew!

Wanting to assuage their unrest over his imprisonment, Paul urges the Philippians that his circumstances have fallen out for the greater progress of the gospel. That word "furtherance" in the KJV, or "turned out" in the NASB is the Greek word from which we get our English word "advance." It is an ancient

Roman military term. It literally means to fall forward. In it is a marvelous picture of the providence of God at work in our difficult moments. He causes His gospel to advance even in the face of adversity.

In antiquity, the word used here for furtherance speaks to the role of Caesar's military advance team. Caesar commissioned a group of engineers and field workers to travel ahead of the Roman army not as a team to fight, but as a means to clear the path of the fighters. By cutting trees, breaking stone, and burning brush, this group literally cleared the path so that the emperor's army and agenda could more easily move forward. Without them, the army carrying his agenda would move but with significant delay.

Paul understands his circumstances, and more specifically his Roman jail time, to be playing the role of the God's advance team. Because of his jail stint, the gospel gets greater progress. Don't miss the adverb greater. The KJV renders it "rather." It is a not so subtle nod that the unstoppable force of the gospel. The gospel, says Paul, is already progressing, and his circumstances are yielding greater progress.

It gets more interesting. His adversity created a new audience for the gospel. The historical context suggests that Paul is chained to a rotating Roman guard. In those days, house arrest prisoners were not monitored by remote devices. They were chained to real-life guards. Catch the distinction in the text. These are not just any guards. These are the famed Praetorian guards. Historians tell us that these guards were imperial watchmen. They were of such rank that they served as bodyguards of the emperor. So influential are they, that the emperor considered their professional satisfaction an antidote to political rebellion. In other words, these men worked house arrest with Rome's political criminals. These are not the beat street cops working the violence prevention program in the Roman ghettos. These guards have noteworthy influence. The prominence is significant to the outworking of this text.

Given that these guards are rotating, it is safe to conclude that with every shift change came a different guard. What do you think they talked about in those close quarters during the shift? With every new imperial guard came a new opportunity for Paul to share the gospel. In my mind I imagine the conversation to have gone something like this:

> Officer: *Hey Mr. Paul, how are you?*
>
> Paul: *I'm fine.*
>
> Officer: *Why are you here?*
>
> Paul: *Have you heard about Jesus?*

We can't be sure, but who knows if these imperial guards were not the men who planted seeds for the softening of Constantine's heart toward the

Christian faith? Who knows if they led to the turn of Rome toward the face of Christ? What we do know is that through this jail stint the gospel reached Caesar's home. Philippians 4:22, tells us that even those from Caesar's household sent their greetings! How about that for a Roman imprisonment?

A few months ago, our children's godparents got an unexpected surprise. What was thought to be vertigo in the godmother turned out to be far worse. Equilibrium off course, walking difficult, vision blurred turned into an emergency room visit. Tests were run and the diagnosis is not good: a brain tumor. In a few short moments, their world was turned inside out. It is the kind of moment when the most carefully laid plans are interrupted. They have a son. He is a gifted and accomplished young man. Though his resume is rich, his faith had not quite caught up. Upon hearing the news of her circumstance, he phones his dad at the bedside of his mother. His words are chilling. He says, "Dad, I know you know God. I need you to pray and ask Him to take care of Mom." Hearing her husband in conversation with their son, the mother reached for the phone and said, 'Son, I know Dad knows how to pray; but, maybe God has let this happen to me so that your faith will get strong." She echoed the encouragement of this text by saying 'my circumstances are turning out for the benefit of your faith.'

Whatever you face, God knows how to use it for the advancement of His gospel. A sickness? There is a doctor who needs to know Jesus. A pink slip? There is a co-worker who needs to know Jesus. A disconnection notice? There are some children watching who need to know Jesus. A wayward child? A broken relationship? Whatever it may be, God could be using your circumstances as a catalyst to achieve His work in the world.

This text is not only an encouragement in the face of adversity. It is also a word of warning against immature discipleship. This text says something about the priority of our convictions over and against the priority of our personal comfort. Paul's interpretation of his circumstances flies in the face of our easy do-ism brand of faith today. He argues that authentic discipleship will cost you personal comfort. Many churchgoers have a tailor-made, Christ-less Christianity. It is a kind of Burger-King Christianity where the Christian gets to have it their way. Yet this text teaches us that the same Jesus who is willingly our Savior simultaneously demands that He be our Lord.

This is not some morbid mantra, but it is a mark of matriculation. It is a sign of growth. Let me be careful not to misrepresent Paul. He is not experiencing joy because he is in jail. This is joy from what being in jail is doing for the gospel!

Enemies are encouragers not impediments

Paul's circumstances advanced the gospel both within and without the church. There were two types of people affected by Paul's chains. First, there were those who were motivated by mercy. Those who appreciated Paul's ministry. His adversity produced courage in those who needed an example. Then there are those who were motivated by misery. His adversity unveiled the hatred of those who needed an excuse.

In this instance, those motivated by misery are the Judaizers. These men were a sect of Jewish religious devotees. Their concern was that Christianity threatened the demise of Judaism. Thinking to cause Paul distress, they preached Christ when he could not. Notice that the text says they preached from envy and strife. Envy is that inward, invisible, intangible resentfulness that precedes strife. Strife is the outward, visible, tangible expression of bitterness. Where there is envy, strife is soon to follow. They preached the right content with the wrong motivation. They exclaimed the name of Christ for the wrong reasons. It is to say to us that our motivation for gospel proclamation ought to be congruent with the message we preach.

The language of distress in Philippians 1:17 means to tighten the grip of the chains. Yet their preaching had the opposite effect on Paul. The natural response is dejection and disappointment. Paul rejoices. So long as they are preaching Christ, he keeps on rejoicing. This is why we can see our enemies as encouragers and not impediments.

God uses the mal-intent of others to achieve His high and holy plans. God permits what He hates to achieve what He loves. The goal is for you and I to see our enemies as tools of God and not obstacles for frustration.

The mythical legend Hercules helps me to illustrate this. When Hercules wrestled with Antaeus he found that every time he threw him down upon the ground the enemy arose stronger than before. But when he discovered that Gaea – the Earth – was the mother of the giant, and that every time her son fell back upon her bosom he rose with renewed strength, then Hercules changed his tactics. Lifting Antaeus high in the air, away from the source of strength, he held him there till he brought him into subjection.

We, who are not children of Earth but children of God, could learn much from the lesson of Antaeus. We, too, whenever troubles cast us back upon the bosom of our Father, rise with renewed strength. But just as Antaeus let Hercules, who was smaller in stature than he, lift him away from the source of his power, so may circumstances, infinitely small and trivial, drag us away from God. Enemies, troubles, misfortunes, disappointments, and handicaps, if they but throw us back upon God, cease to be evil and become good. Joseph understood that later in his life. Your enemies can be either impediments to progress or they can be instruments of progress.

Joy is consequential not circumstantial

Lastly, Paul argues that joy is consequential not circumstantial. He declares his resolve to rejoice. Then he states the reason for his resolution.

Paul's rejoicing is a result of the proclamation of Jesus Christ. Oh for more Christians to love and rejoice in the proclamation of Jesus Christ! We have switched joy distributors in our postmodern Western context. We have exchanged the eternal joy of Christ for the temporal excitement of possessions. This text says that there is something about the message of Christ that produces joy in the hearts of those who love his name.

We need a revival of preaching Jesus in our churches. That is where real joy is found. We need to tell people that he was born of a virgin with stable for a crib. We need to tell them that in eternity he rested on the bosom of his father without a mother, and in time he rested on his mother without an earthly father. We need tell them that he is as old as his father and ages older than his mother. We need to tell them that He is sin's recompense, the sinner's way home, and the balm for brokenness. When all else fails, we can tell them that He is still bread for the hungry, water for the thirsty and the only way to the Father. Then they will have joy.

BEATING THE GIANTS THAT BEAT OUR FATHERS
Anthony Chandler
Joshua 14: 12-15

Just a few weeks ago, while sitting in the waiting room of a doctor's office, there was an elderly white man sitting next to me as we were watching the flat screen television positioned on the wall. As we were both watching the news and report after report after report, each seemed to be worse than the last. This elderly man looked at me and began to strike up a conversation. He said to me, *"I long for the day when we will turn on the new and all of the news will be good news."*

Friends, it seems that we are now living in a world where no place is a safe place. Elementary schools, as evidenced of the 20 small children who were killed at Sandyhook Elementary School last year, are no longer safe. Running in a marathon is no longer safe. Sitting in a movie theater with your friends and family is no longer safe and, if it were not already difficult enough to get Christians to come to Bible Study and regular attendance on Sunday mornings, who would have ever thought that attending Bible Study or a mid-week worship, would become the place of your demise.

We are living, as author Charles Dickens said, *"In the best of times... and in the worst of times."* In the words of Thomas Paine, one of our founding fathers, *"These are times, that try men's souls."*

However, as a man of God, as a congregation of believers, and as a children of the Most High God, we still must stand firm in the precepts and on the principles of our faith and be well assured, that **no matter what is happening in our world today, our God is still in control.**

Even when our hearts are heavy, **God is still in control.**

Even when we experience life situations that literally take our breath away, **God is still in control.**

Even in the most dark situation, **God is still in control,** ***and we must trust Him!***

Because, in Bible that we read it says, *what the devil meant for evil, He will make it work for my good.* In my Bible, it reads, *Though a host should* encamp *around me my heart shall not fear though war should rise up against me in this will I be confident.* In my Bible, it reads, *Many are the afflictions of the righteous but the Lord shall deliver them from them all.*

In my Bible, it reads, *I've been young and now I'm old and I've never seen the righteous forsaken!* In the Bible that I read, it says, *That the name of the Lord is a strong tower the righteous run in and they are safe.*

For many of us, our hearts may be broken, and fear, for some, has manifested itself, but friends, we do not worry as those who have no hope. We will not live in fear and we will not be divided, **but we will trust in the God of our salvation!**

That's why I believe you came to church. You came because in your heart, you understood that you couldn't find your answer on CNN or MSNBC. No one on FOXnews can relate to what you are going through.

Nevertheless, somebody said, *"That when my heart is overwhelmed, lead me to the rock that's higher than I."*

- Because, there is safety in the rock.
- There is protection in the rock.
- There is joy in the rock.
- There is healing in the rock.
- There is deliverance in the rock.
- There is forgiveness in the rock.
- There is salvation in the rock.
- There is peace in the rock.

Friends, I don't know about you, but I'm glad to be in this church for multiple reasons. One reason I'm glad is because it is my birthday, and I'm happy to be alive. Secondly, I'm here because I'm determined to let the devil know that no matter what he tries to do in my life, he will not keep me from coming to church!

As a matter of fact, if I have to die – if the devil just has to take me out of here – he needs to know that the best time/place to take me out is while I'm serving my God and/or as I'm studying God's Word. Because *"if I perish, let me perish! Because I'm standing firm on what I believe that to be absent from this body means that I am present with the Lord!"*

Those saintly people in South Carolina exemplified true Christianity. My heart just like your heart was in shock and disbelief but then I thought about something. Death is not the ending for a saint, it is really a new beginning. Because, when you think about the basis and the foundation of our faith – and maybe you have forgotten about this – but our faith all began because somebody decided to die! On a hill far away stood an old rugged cross, the emblem of suffering and shame.

So don't you think that the crisis in South Carolina will be in vain and the devil is a liar? Sometimes it takes a crisis to wake up a community. Sometimes it takes a crisis to bring people together. Sometimes it takes a crisis to bring folk to church! Sometimes it takes a crisis to win folk to Christ!

Sometimes it takes a crisis for black folk and white folk, old folk and young folk, rich folk and broke folk, educated folk and mis-educated folk, folk from the county and people who live in the city to stand up and declare, ***Together we stand for divided we fall!!***

In our text, we are introduced to Caleb. Caleb was a father, a fighter and a family man. Bible students are not hearing about him for the first time, for they heard about him back in the book of Numbers (chapter 13), when the Lord told Moses to send 12 men to search the land of Canaan. Twelve men, twelve spies, if you would went sent out to survey the land. It was a land promised to their fathers, the descendants of Abraham. Supposedly, when they saw the land, they saw a land flowing with milk and honey. For 40 days, they scouted out the land. They said, *"Pastor Moses we've seen this land and we have some good news and some bad news. The good news Sir is that this land is filled with promising possibilities. It was indeed a land flowing with milk and honey. We can see why our fathers wanted us to have this land. We've even brought you a piece of fruit. Taste and see for yourself. There's some good fruit in that land. However, Pastor Moses, we also have some bad news. This land is good, but the only thing wrong with the land is that in order for us to conquer the land, we've got to overtake the people who live there. But here is the problem. The men there are HUGE! I mean they are giants. They are like creatures from Jurassic Park."*

As ten of the twelve were speaking, Joshua and Caleb, two of the twelve, with Caleb being the leading spokesperson, interjected and said, *"Hold up...wait a minute. Why yall scared? I saw the same land that you saw. And....yes, I saw the same giants that you saw, but I ain't scared...we can do this!*

Caleb is a man and certainly a father to be admired. The Bible says that the other men said, *"We can't do this!"* But Caleb was like Lebron James. He was saying, *"We can do this, but I can't be the only one trying to win this game. Can you help a brother out?"*

And now, it is 45 years later. At the age of eighty-five, Caleb says, *"...lets revisit"* this thing one more time and, in this 14th chapter of Joshua, notice he is not making a request, he is making a demand!

God told me to tell you that for your next move – for your next miracle – you can't walk in the room asking. You've got to make your request known and say, *"this is what I want and this what I'm going to get! And, I'm not leaving until I get it!"*

Someone needs to tell his/her supervisor that, with all due respect, "I will not work and not be paid what I'm deserved. I will not be overlooked or ignored. The same way that you look out for your friends, you are going to look out for me."

Someone is in a relationship that you are sharing with another person, but you must declare, "I will not be in a relationship where I am the other one. Either I will be the only one, or I'm on to the next one…to the left, to the left!"

This is not the season for you to settle or accept what others want or think you should have? They don't know all that you've been through. They don't know all the nights you've cried. They don't know all the pain you've endured.

You need to remind somebody that I don't serve a halfway God; I don't have a halfway faith; I don't read a halfway Bible; I don't attend a halfway church and when I come to church, I don't come with a halfway praise.

I'm not like some of these people who get happy when they feel like it. They waive their hands…when they feel like it. They clap for joy…when they feel like it, and they stand up and say amen…..when they feel like it.

I am not a halfway worshipper. With my whole heart, I praise Him! With my whole heart, I bless Him! With my whole heart, I serve Him! When I think of the goodness of Jesus and all that He has done for me, my soul cries *Hallelujah,* and I thank God for saving me..

Caleb said, *"Give me this mountain!*

Let me share with you three things that you have to do to get to your promise land and to conquer the land that our fathers never defeated.

1. DON'T ALLOW FEAR TO KEEP YOU FROM YOUR FUTURE

According to the Bible, the other spies couldn't move forward because of fear. They could only see themselves as grasshoppers. What they didn't understand was this: *as a man thinketh in his heart, so is he.*

That's why you've got to watch the words that come out of your mouth. Your words have power. If you see yourself as a loser, you've already declared defeat. If you see yourself as broke, busted and disgusted, you will always need a hand up or a hand out. And, if you see yourself as the victim, you will never be victorious.

My friends don't you know that life and death is in the power.... of your tongue! What I love about Caleb was that when the other men saw themselves as grasshoppers, Caleb was like *"speak for yourself!"*

For you see, the ten spies compared the giants with or to themselves; but Caleb compared the giants to his God. The ten spies saw the giants, but all Caleb could see was his God!

Friends when you are going through a situation that you never thought or imagined you'd be in, take a moment and look for God! Because – whether you believe it or not – He's there! Yes, He's there! When I was a younger preacher, I used to say

- God is like Coca-Cola. He's the real thing!
- God is like General Electric. He lights your path.
- God is like Bayer Aspirin. He works wonders.
- God is like Hallmark cards. He cared enough to send the very best.
- God is like Tide...He gets the stains out that others leave behind.
- God is like Dial soap. Aren't you glad you know Him? Don't you wish everybody everybody did?
- God is like Sears...He has everything.
- God is like Alka Seltzer. Oh, what a relief He is.
- God is like Scotch tape. You can't see Him, but you know He's there.

I used to say that all of that and much more when I was a younger preacher. But now I'm 42 years old and much more mature than I once was. I can now say, I've been a lot of places. I've see alot of faces. There have been times when I felt so all alone, but in my lonely hours. Yes, those precious lonely hours. Jesus, let me know that I was His own.

I thank God for the mountains. I thank God for the valleys. I thank Him for the storms He's brought me through. For if I'd never had a problem, I would not know God could solve them. I would never know what faith in God could do. But now, I can say,

Through it all... *"Thank you Jesus!"*

Number one....don't allow fear to keep you from your future.

2. DON'T ALLOW FAILURE TO REMAIN A FACTOR

Caleb is now 85 years old. Understand this, the plan failed 45 years prior, but for 45 years now, Caleb couldn't get this thing out of his mind. Forty-five years ago, Caleb had a plan, and now the plan has changed.

I know you don't like to be honest with yourself, but like many of us – where we are right now is not where we want or thought we would be. Now, all we can say is that somewhere down the road, the plan changed or it failed. Not too long ago it seemed like everything was almost picture perfect.

Your money was in order. Your family was in order. Your dreams were in order. Your career was in order. Your health was in good standing. Your credit got you in the door. Your friends had your back. And your circle was never expected to be broken but somewhere down the road, things changed. The plan changed or it failed!

Now, your money is at an all time low. Your family is working your nerves at an all time high. Your dreams have almost turned into nightmares. Your career has turned into a job you really don't like. Your health is questionable, and you don't even like going to the doctor; and your credit is so bad that when they try to run your credit, alarms sound.

Now you are sitting in church and all you can say is this, *"somehow, some way, the plan changed. The plan failed."* If you are able to look back over your life, and see that where you thought you would be, you are not there right now. What you thought you would have, you don't have right now. And, you are dealing with a plethora of things that were not supposed to happen:

- the death wasn't supposed to happen.
- the divorce wasn't supposed to happen.
- the demotion wasn't supposed to happen.
- the diagnosis wasn't supposed to happen.
- the deadline wasn't supposed to happen.
- the delay wasn't supposed to happen.
- the defeat wasn't supposed to happen.
- the deceit wasn't supposed to happen.
- the dismissal wasn't supposed to happen.

And today, all you can say is that somewhere down the road, the plan changed. Since the plan has changed, it seems like you have lost sight, your view, your perspective and your hope. There are even days when it looks like you've failed.

But I bring you good news! Your plans may have changed, but God is still the same! The good news is that the Bible says God's promises are *yes* and *amen!* If the Lord said it, I don't care what others have said. I don't care what others have told you; and I don't care what other people think about you.

Even if you have failed or fallen, the Bible says, in Psalm 24:16, *that a righteous man falleth seven times, but rises up again.* And friends, I don't care how old you are; how wrinkled you are; how bruised you are; how defeated you may feel; or how long it has taken you to get to this place. The good news today is you are still alive!

In the game of chess, you may hear the word *Check* a dozen times, but as long as you don't hear the words *Checkmate*, that means your King...... still has another move! 4And if you don't remember anything else that I have said, please remember this, "My king still has another move! I don't care what your doctor said, "my king still has another move." I don't care what your lawyer said; I don't care what your counselor said; I don't care what the loan officer said; and I don't care what your boss said. My King still has another move!

If we are going to beat the giants that beat our fathers, we cannot allow fear to keep us from our future. We cannot allow failure to remain a factor. But finally, whatever you do:

3. DON'T FORGET TO STAND FIRM IN YOUR FAITH

What I like about Caleb was that Caleb, he wasn't a chump. He told Joshua, "I'm old, but I'm still alive. And I am as strong today, as I was 45 years ago. In verse 12, he also said, *"I don't care how big these giants are; this is what I know: God is with me!"* Caleb said, *"Give me this mountain!"* And, according to the text, he received it all because he stood firm in his faith.

Friends, in times of fear and during seasons of worry and uncertainty, you've got to remain firm in your faith!

Sometimes you've got to just be still and know that God is with you. David said, *"Trust in the Lord, and lean not to your own understanding. In all your ways, acknowledge him, and He will direct your paths."*

I hear the Spirit of God saying, "Don't give up!" I know it's hard, but don't give up. I know it hurts, but don't give up. I know they are doing you wrong, but don't give up. I know they want you quit, but don't give up. And, don't listen to what everybody else is telling you to do. They don't even have what you have. How are they going to tell you how to manage your relationship and they don't have anybody?

Stand firm in your faith; stand firm in what you believe because there is a blessing coming. One day you can say like Paul, *"I've fought a good fight. I've finished my course. I've kept the faith!"*

A story is told of a little boy who was trapped in the basement of his house while a fire was in progress upstairs. But the boy had faith because his grandmother had taught him about the Lord. He found some books over in the corner. One was an encyclopedia. One was a dictionary. He placed them on top of a chair in order to stand on them to reach the window…..in order to open it up and escape. However, even while standing on the encyclopedia and standing on the dictionary, he still could not reach the window. He began to pray that said, "Lord, please make a way!"

After he prayed, he looked over in the corner and in the corner, he saw the family Bible on another book shelf. Then, he remembered what his grandmother told him. One day she told him, "Son, if you stand on the Word, the Word will stand for you!" He took the Bible and placed it on the top of the other books, and then he stood on it. And when he stood on the Bible, he was able to reach the window and climbed out safely.

When you stand on God's Word - in times of trials, He will allow you to reach a window of opportunity. Stand on His Word and keep the faith!!! After you've done all you can, just stand!

God has another move; so keep the faith. He will give you strength; so keep the faith. He will make a way; so keep the faith. He will work it out; so keep the faith. He will keep you in perfect peace; so keep the faith; and He will fight my battles!

It is time for us to beat these giants! The giants of Racism; The giants of Sexism; The giants of classism; The giants of hatred; The giants of inequality; and the giants of envy! Let's kill these giants!

And I'm so glad that my God is a giant killer. Jesus was a giant killer. He destroyed the giant of sin. He destroyed the giant of a cross. He destroyed the giant of hatred. He destroyed the giant of death. He destroyed that giant of a grave. All, because He took a stand!

You Can't Tell Me What Prayer Can't Do
E. Winford Bell
2 Kings 20:1-2

Do you remember the old saying, "When it rains, it pours," or "You just can't win for losing"? I can imagine that Hezekiah felt like that. (For his county was being invaded; he was sick, and he had no successor.)

You must understand that, on a very real note, this passage of Scripture deals with information or news that comes to an individual that he or she may or may not want to hear. Yet, God has a way of getting the Word to us, whether we want it or not!

Some people get upset at the mailman for bringing us bad news, but it is not the mailman that causes you to feel anger, it is the information in the letter.

These days, we have gotten more sophisticated in avoiding bad news. If there is a knock on the door, some of us will look through the window and not answer; if the phone rings, the answering machine or voicemail can pick it up; if you don't want mail to come to your house, you can just get a P.O. Box at the post office. Many of us just don't want to hear or face any bad news.

But what should you really do when bad news comes into your life? There is what is known as prayer. What is prayer? Well, it is a combination of things tied into one knot. First, and foremost, it is a direct line of communication that comes from man to God. It is God's way of allowing us to talk to Him to ask what we will.

For the most part, fervent prayers, those ones that you've heard people say, "that man sho' did say his prayer." Fervent prayer comes out the 4 T's (as I call them): Testing, Tribulation, Troubles, and Trials. We all go through them. If you haven't, just keep on living!

Testing

Abraham was tested. God told Abraham, "to take thy son, thy only son Isaac, and make him an offering, a burnt offering." Job had everything a man could ever think to have: children, land, sheep, oxen, and money. Job was rich. Yet, Satan told God to take the hedge from around him and "I'll make him curse you!" *God will test you!*

Some of you are being tested right now. You've been entrusted with position of authority in work places, and even in church, and the temptations to do wrong is always present. "For whenever I desire to do good, evil is always present."

Tribulation is to deal with great affixation, great pain, and suffering of both mind & body. Jesus said you would suffer great tribulation for my namesake.

Trouble is when you get that daughter straight, the son starts; when you get him straight, then it's husband, or the wife. Trouble, trouble, trouble!

Trials will show you that, "If ain't one thing, it's another!"

Somehow when you're going through something, whatever you're saying or asking has more depth to it. It has more power to it, more feeling to it.

Unlike if you have no difficulties in life. When you have no problems, no hard times, or trials, prayer becomes weak. They become cold. They just don't come from the heart.

So I'm led to believe that even though I've had many tears and sorrow, I've had questions for tomorrow. I didn't know right from wrong; but in every situation God gives me blessed consolation to let these trials come to make me strong!

There are problems in life that we just cannot handle. Our understanding is too limited, our physical might is too weak, our arms are too short, our legs are too slow, our eyes are too dim to see the distance, and our backs cannot carry the load. But even knowing this, there are those who will still say, "I'm going to help God out! God's moving a little slow!" Every time we get self in the way, self will mess it up.

God has His set time when He shall move! It may be in the morning, it may be in the noonday, or it may be at night. It may not be when I want it. He may not come when I say, but my God is always right on time!

God told Sarah she would conceive in her old age, and she got impatient. It didn't happen when she thought it should. She sent Abraham to Hagar and that caused her own jealousy. At a set time Moses was to come down from Mt. Sinai, but the children of Israel got impatient and started making idol gods. At a set time Jonah was to go to Nineveh, but chose to do differently and ended up in a belly of a whale.

You cannot hurry God! You cannot rush God! He will move at His set time.

At a set time, Sodom and Gomorrah were destroyed. At a set time, Israel was delivered. At a set time, water came from the rock in the wilderness. At a set time, manna fell from on high. At a set time, Samuel anointed David as king. David killed Goliath. Elisha received Elijah's mantle and carried on.

At a set time, God shall cut down the worker of iniquity; He'll put your enemies under your feet. At a set time, He shall deliver you, fight for you. God does things in His time.

That is why we must say as Isaiah said, *"they that wait upon the Lord shall renew their strength; they shall mount up with wings as eagles; they shall run, and not be weary; and they shall walk, and not faint."*

So it was with Hezekiah, he did what we should do. When we can't handle it, when we can't fix it. Have a little talk with Jesus, tell Him all about your trouble, He'll hear your faintest cry and answer by and by.

We are to turn our face to the wall...get to our secret place, and pray! Every second, minute, hour, day, week, month, down through the year, we need to pray just to be able to make it today. He'll answer prayer. He gave Hezekiah fifteen years.

Daniel prayed. Shadrach, Meshach, and Abednego prayed. Samson prayed, *"Lord give me the strength!"* Jesus prayed, *"Father forgive them."* The church prayed for Peter. Paul and Silas prayed. No matter what, stay in touch with God.

Pray and God will answer!

Contributors

Reverend E. Winford Bell
The Reverend Dr. E. Winford Bell, is the Senior Pastor of the Mt. Olive Second Missionary Baptist Church in Los Angeles, CA. Pastor Bell was presented with an Honorary Doctorate of Divinity Degree, from the Inglewood Bible College of Evangelical Seminary. On July 15, 2015, Pastor Bell completed his 4 year tenure as President of the Progressive Baptist State Convention of California. In July 1986, Rev. Bell married the love of his life, Maria Elena Howard, who stands lovingly by his side and encourages and supports the growth of his ministry. Rev. Bell has four children and five grandchildren.

Reverend Charles E. Booth
The Reverend Dr. Charles E. Booth is the Senior Pastor of Mt Olivet Baptist Church in Columbus, Ohio. He earned his Bachelor of Arts degree at Howard University and his Master of Divinity degree from Eastern Theological Seminary in Philadelphia, Pennsylvania. He earned the Doctor of Ministry degree from United Theological Seminary in Dayton, Ohio where he serves as a member of the Board of Trustees. Dr. Booth serves as an affiliate professor of homiletics at the Trinity Lutheran Seminary in Columbus, Ohio. Dr. Booth's biography and a sermon appear in Preaching with **Sacred Fire: An Anthology of African-American Sermons, 1750-Present.** His most recent publication is **Stronger In my Broken Places** (MMGI Books).

Reverend Delores James Cain
The Reverend Dr. Delores James Cain is the organizer and Pastor of Heritage Christian Community Baptist Church of Lutz, Florida. She is a native of Chicago Illinoism and the daughter of a Baptist pastor. Rev. Cain works as a private consultant in the area of child welfare. She holds a bachelor's degree in sociology from the University of Illinois and a Master of Social work degree from Florida State University in Tallahassee and was awarded an Honorary Doctor of Ministry in 2013 from the Richmond Virginia Seminary in Richmond VA and received a Doctor of Ministry degree, as a William Curtis/Gina Stewart Fellow in 2014 from the United Theological Seminary, in Dayton Ohio.

Reverend Anthony M. Chandler
A Baltimore native, the Reverend Dr. Anthony Michael Chandler is the distinguished pastor of the Cedar Street Baptist Church in Richmond, Virginia. He graduated from United Theological Seminary in 2003 earning the Doctor of Ministry degree. In 2014, he earned a MBA from Virginia Commonwealth University. He is married to Dr. Taleshia Chandler and they are the proud parents of Anthony II, Alysha and Andrew.

Reverend Charlie Dates
In 2011, at age 30, the Reverend Charlie Edward Dates became the youngest Senior Pastor in Progressive's rich 95-year history. Rev. Charlie earned a Bachelor of Arts in Speech Communication and Rhetoric at the University of Illinois at Urbana-Champaign and a Master of Divinity Degree at Trinity Evangelical Divinity School in Deerfield, Illinois. He currently is a candidate for the PhD in Historical Theology at Trinity Evangelical Divinity School. Pastor Charlie is married to Kirstie Dates and is the proud father of their children Charlie Edward Dates II and Claire Elisabeth Dates.

Reverend Willie R. Davis
The Reverend Willie R. Davis currently serves as the Senior Pastor/Founder of MacGregor Palm Community Baptist Church in Houston, Texas. He is the Past President At Large of the Progressive National Baptist Convention, Southwest Region. He attended Sam Houston State University of Huntsville, Texas and received his Masters of Theology from Texas School of Theology in Houston Texas. He is married to Michelle B. Davis.

Reverend Kenneth J. Flowers
The Reverend Kenneth James Flowers is Senior Pastor of Greater New Mt. Moriah Missionary Baptist Church in Detroit, Michigan. He is Immediate Past President of Michigan Progressive Baptist Convention, Inc. He serves as National Chair of the Evangelism Board for Progressive National Baptist Convention, Inc. He is a Graduate of Morehouse College in Atlanta, Georgia and Colgate Rochester Crozer Divinity School, in Rochester, New York. He is currently a Gardner C. Taylor Doctoral Student at United Theological Seminary in Dayton, Ohio. He's the father of three wonderful daughters Kierra Tenine, Kaletah Marie, and Kristiana Rose.

Reverend Tyrone P. Jones IV
The Reverend Tyrone P. Jones IV is the Pastor of the historic First Baptist Church of Guilford, Columbia, MD since 2011. Pastor Jones has been preaching the gospel for 20 years, and has served as a pastor for 14 years. Pastor Jones hails from Augusta, GA. He holds an M.Div from Howard University and a Th.M from Princeton Seminary. He is currently a D.Min candidate at Colgate Rochester Crozer Divinity School.

Reverend Marvin A. McMickle
Marvin A. McMickle, Ph.D. is the 12th president of Colgate Rochester Crozer Divinity School in Rochester, New York. Prior to coming to Rochester he spent 34 years as a pastor in New Jersey and Ohio. He has taught preaching at Ashland Theological Seminary, Princeton Theological Seminary and Yale University Divinity School. He is the author of 15 books and numerous journal articles and book chapters. He and his wife Peggy have been married since 1975. They have one son, Aaron who lives with his family in Brooklyn, New York.

Reverend Earl B. Payton
The Reverend Earl B. Payton is the Founding Pastor of Sun City Christian Fellowship Baptist Church in El Paso, Texas He served 30 years as an Army Chaplain, and is a distinguished Bronze Star Retiree. He is the immediate Past President of the Progressive National Baptist Southwest Region. Rev. Pastor Chairs the Board of Directors of the Sun City Development Corporation a 501 (c) (3) corporation.

Reverend James C. Perkins
The Reverend Dr. James C. Perkins has served as pastor of Greater Christ Baptist Church in Detroit, Michigan for thirty-three years. He currently serves as the President of The Progressive Baptist Convention, Inc. He is the author of **Building Up Zion's Walls: Ministry for Empowering the African American Family** and **Playbook for Christian Manhood: 12 Key Plays for Black Teen Boys**, published by Judson Press. Responding to the crisis he witnessed in the available educational options for young, urban African American males, Dr. Perkins instituted the Benjamin E. Mays Male Academy in 1993. This kindergarten through sixth grade Christian school for boys operated for 17 years and positively impacted the future of hundreds of males. Dr. Perkins is married to Linda Adkins Perkins and is the father of two daughters and the grandfather of one grandson.

Reverend William H. Robinson
In 2012, the Reverend Dr. William H. Robinson was selected as the third Pastor of The Olivet Church in Fayetteville, Georgia. Dr. Robinson answered the call to the ministry while he was a student at Morehouse College and under the leadership of Pastor Timothy Fleming was ordained and licensed to preach in 1994. In 1997, he completed his Bachelor of Arts degree in Religion from Morehouse College. Dr. Robinson received his Master of Divinity in 2000 and his Doctorate of Ministry in 2009 from the Morehouse School of Religion at the Interdenominational Theological Center.

Reverend Gina M. Stewart
The Reverend Dr. Gina Marcia Stewart has led the congregation of Christ Missionary Baptist Church since March 1995. She earned a Bachelor of Business Administration in Marketing in 1982 from the University of Memphis. In 1989, she received a Master of Education in Administration and Supervision from Trevecca Nazarene College in Nashville, Tennessee. She received the Master of Divinity degree from Memphis Theological Seminary in May 1996. Rev. Stewart also attended the Harvard Divinity School Summer Leadership Institute for Church Based Community and Economic Development (2000). She received the Doctor of Ministry degree from the ITC-Interdenominational Theological Center-(ITC)-Atlanta, Georgia on May 5, 2007.

Reverend Jacqueline A. Thompson
The Reverend Dr. Jacqueline A. Thompson is the Assistant Pastor of The Historic Allen Temple Baptist Church in Oakland, California, the first woman to serve in this capacity. She is a graduate of Howard University School of Divinity and Fuller Theological Seminary. She currently serves as Chair of the Planning and Evaluation Committee of the Progressive National Baptist Convention, Inc.

Reverend Raphael G. Warnock
The Reverend Dr. Raphael Gamaliel Warnock has served, since 2005, as the Senior Pastor of the historic Ebenezer Baptist Church. Dr. Warnock graduated from Morehouse College cum laude in 1991, receiving the B.A. degree in psychology. He also holds a Master of Divinity (M.Div.) degree from Union Theological Seminary, New York City, from which he graduated with honors and distinctions. Rev. Warnock continued his graduate studies at Union, receiving a Master of Philosophy (M.Phil.) degree and a Doctor of Philosophy (Ph.D.) degree in the field of systematic theology. His first book is entitled, **The Divided Mind of the Black Church; Theology, Piety & Public Witness** *(NYU Press, 2014).*

Reverend Johnny Ray Youngblood
Since May 2001, the Reverend Dr. Johnny Ray Youngblood has been serving as the Executive Pastor of the Mount Pisgah Baptist Church, Brooklyn, New York. Before 2001, Youngblood had spent 35 years (1974-2009) at the St. Paul Community Baptist Church in Brooklyn, New York. Dr. Youngblood has earned a Bachelors ~ Dillard University, New Orleans, LA; Masters of Divinity ~ Colgate Rochester Divinity School-Crozer Theological Seminary, Rochester NY; Doctorate of Ministry ~ United Theological Seminary, Dayton OH Youngblood is the father of three sons, Johnny Jernell, Joel Ray and Jason Royce, and grandfather of Donnalyn, Joshua, Jalen, Jordyn, Jasmine and Nicholas.